Praise for *7-Figure Educator*

"What makes 7-Figure Educator powerful is its clarity. Dr. Erica Jordan-Thomas combines lived experience, proven strategy, and cultural competence into a business framework educators can actually execute. This book belongs on the desk of every educator serious about entrepreneurship and ownership."
— Lamar Tyler, Co-Founder & CEO, Traffic, Sales & Profit

"This book offers a candid examination of what it can mean for educators to rethink the boundaries of their work and influence. 7-Figure Educator brings clarity and intention to questions of agency, leadership, and long-term sustainability."
— Nancy Gutierrez, Ed.L.D., President & CEO, The Leadership Academy

"7-Figure Educator is a must-read for educators who want to expand their influence, income, and impact. Dr. Erica has a rare gift for breaking down big ideas into clear, actionable steps that help educators feel seen, capable, and empowered to build something bigger than the classroom."
— Teri Ijeoma, Founder, Trade & Travel

"7-Figure Educator gives educators permission to imagine more. Dr. Erica Jordan-Thomas delivers a strategic, mindset-shifting framework for transforming expertise into agency, wealth, and purpose-driven enterprise."
— Elisa Villanueva Beard, Former CEO, Teach For America, President & CEO, Houston Endowment

7-Figure Educator

7-Figure Educator

TURN YOUR EXPERIENCE as an EDUCATOR into INCOME, IMPACT, and FREEDOM

DR. ERICA JORDAN-THOMAS

HAY HOUSE LLC

Carlsbad, California • New York City
London • Sydney • New Delhi

CONTENTS

Introduction

When I started my business back in 2017, I was trying to prove something to myself.

As a teacher, my salary was $33,000 a year. I remember thinking, *What if I could figure out how to make in one month what I used to make in a whole year?*

That number—$33,000—became my North Star. It was taped to my vision board, it was the number I whispered in prayer, it was the bar I measured myself against every single month.

And the day I finally hit it? Whew. I sat in front of my laptop in disbelief, because it wasn't just about the money—it was about proof. Proof that I wasn't crazy for leaving a "safe" salary. Proof that the sacrifice was worth it. Proof that God really did put this vision in me for a reason.

Here's the wild thing about goals: When you finally reach them, the ceiling starts shifting. That ceiling that felt so high at the time . . . it's now my floor. Writing this less than 10 years later, I sometimes spend $33,000 in a day. Now, don't get it twisted. Back in 2017, if you would've told me I'd casually spend more in a day than I used to earn in a year, I would've laughed you out of the room. I'm sharing this with you not to brag but rather to demonstrate the power of entrepreneurship. What I know today after helping thousands of educators to create their own wealth is that when you stay committed to the work, when you keep showing up even when it doesn't feel glamorous, when you trust yourself (and your higher power, if that speaks to you) enough to keep dreaming bigger, you will go places you couldn't have imagined before.

Sometimes "bigger" doesn't just look like hitting new goals. Sometimes "bigger" looks like the old goals becoming your new floor. So, as you start this book, I encourage you to consider—what ceilings are you willing to turn into floors? Because the truth is, the journey of entrepreneurship is never really about the money. Instead, the reward is in the stretch, in the growth, in discovering who you have to become to receive more and achieve what you deserved all along.

In 2023, I hosted my annual event, 7-Figure Educator LIVE. My team and I handed out T-shirts we had created to every attendee. We didn't tell anyone to wear them. But over the next three days, everywhere I looked, people were proudly walking around wearing shirts that read, "If anybody deserves to be a millionaire, it's an educator."

That's when it hit me. That T-shirt wasn't just merch. It wasn't a cute tagline or even a way to promote what I do; I had accidentally started a movement. A movement of educators believing that we deserve wealth. That we deserve respect. And the freedom that comes with both.

But I didn't start out believing any of that.

Instead, I started out as an underpaid, overworked educator. Sound familiar?

Let's wind the clock all the way back. I grew up in Columbus, Ohio, attending predominantly Black public schools. When I went to college, I majored in textile and clothing because I wanted to work in the fashion industry. Specifically, I wanted to be a buyer or a merchandiser, which is a position in a retail company that predicts and forecasts trends in order to buy inventory to sell in stores. But I graduated college in 2008, when the economy crashed and companies were laying off instead of hiring. All my friends were having trouble getting jobs, so I decided to pivot.

I became a teacher.

As it turns out, I was great at teaching math to high schoolers. Despite being new, I had 96 percent student proficiency and I was nominated as best new teacher for my district of 150+ schools. After a few years teaching, I decided to make the jump into leadership. After a year working as an instructional coach and completing New Leaders, a principal-preparation program, I became the assistant principal at Ranson I. B. Middle School in Charlotte, North Carolina. I was promoted to principal of that school at 28 years old, and at the time, North Carolina was ranked last in all 50 states for principal pay. My salary as a principal leading more than 1,000 middle school students was $70,000—roughly $5,800 a month. Even though I was struggling financially, I was able to accomplish a lot of beautiful things during my tenure as principal. Thanks to a combined effort of community, teachers, and school leaders, we were able to take Ranson I. B. from one of the most unsafe schools to being ranked in the top one percent for the state for our student growth.

I want to pause here because I am going to share and specifically think aloud the meta moments—the individual shifts, the key decisions, the relationships—that helped me on my journey to where I am today. Grab your highlighter and notebook or your mental pen so that you can take note of where my story and yours overlap, rhyme, echo. I want you to truly see our many similarities, because I believe that once you are exposed to what is possible, you never forget *that's possible for you*. Let my success and the success of the educators within these pages inspire you, guide your path, and give you proof that your goals, dreams, and big ambitions are possible. Including and not limited to a million-dollar business, if that's what you want.

Back to my story. The first stage of creating change is cultivating a sense of urgency—and most of the time, that comes from disruption. In my experience, that disruption happens in a moment where you suddenly realize, "I ain't doing this no more." For me, that moment happened a week before my next paycheck. I was down to my last $50, and I knew I wasn't going to make it. So I applied for a loan. Let me be clear—I did not get a loan at a bank.

Instead, I was driving from one of those check-cashing places in the 'hood to my bank so I could deposit the money. I was on my way to deposit the money . . . when I ran out of gas. The principal of the middle school ranked in the top one percent of the state for student growth was sitting on the side of the road, broke in more ways than one. That's when I knew that I couldn't continue to live the way I had been living. Something had to change. So, what did I do?

What any type A, overachiever educator would: I made a spreadsheet.

At the time, spreadsheets provided a sense of control for me, and maybe that's how you feel about them too. Like you can breathe because there's a formula in that little top bar telling you everything is going to be okay. Even if the numbers don't work out. *Especially* then. Am I right, or nah? That day I created a spreadsheet with all my bills and my bank accounts. I promised myself that I would budget carefully enough to make things work. Like a lot of folks, I had always been told that saving was the way to always have enough. But at that point, saving was really hard—I had only a couple hundred dollars left over after paying my bills. I was in my 20s. I wanted to go on weekend trips with friends; I wanted to eat out; I wanted to live my life. But saving was all I knew. I didn't know the alternative—which was to make more money. I had no idea *how impossible it is to budget your way to freedom when you are underpaid.*

Fast-forward to another meta moment. Every six years, the district I worked for would reevaluate the boundary lines for every school in the district. (You may already know where this is going, but in case you don't, I'll tell you.) A district administrator showed up at my school on a Friday and let me know that there was a proposal being reviewed by the school board that would add 400-plus students to my building the following year.

I would receive displaced teachers. Any school leader knows not being able to interview and select your own staff is a recipe for a school culture mess to be cleaned up. There would be no additional support staff—no extra counselors, no extra social workers, nothing. And, of course, I wouldn't be receiving a raise, despite my job becoming instantly more challenging and requiring more of my time. I had worked so hard, our school was growing and improving, and I was being rewarded with more work and the same pay, which so often happens in education. Despite feeling happy and purposeful in my role as a principal—and loving my school with all my heart—I knew there was no way I could stay.

I decided to resign at the end of the school year.

I had a whole school year to decide what my next step would be, but for the first time in my life, I had no plan. I thought I would be a career principal, and because I never considered any other option, I didn't know how to pivot. I had no clue. I decided to start by doing education consulting on the side. As a principal, I had hired consultants before, so I knew I could do the work. Though I had decided I was definitely leaving my job, I recognized that I needed money to do so. I figured I could consult until I knew what I *actually* wanted to do next. The uncertainty was stressful, but looking back, I can see that I needed to be disrupted. I needed the sense of urgency this disruption provided to change, to grow, to do something different, to look beyond the walls of my school. Maybe you feel that way too. Maybe that's why you decided to buy this book.

I officially started my business in October 2017 with the goal I mentioned earlier, which was to make in a month what I made in a year as a teacher ($33,000). I got my very first consulting contract—for a one-day professional development (PD) presentation—within 30 days. Receiving my first invoice felt completely life-changing. I charged $1,600, and even though I totally undercharged, I made in a day what it would have taken me two weeks to make as a principal. If you've been there, you know how revelatory that is. I started to wonder.

If I can make $1,600 in a day . . . I wonder if I can make it in a half day.

Once I made $1,600 in half of a day: *I wonder if I can make it in an hour.*

And once I made $1,600 in an hour, I was like, *I bet I could do this in 30 minutes.*

I kept going.

Within the next year, I made $38,000 consulting while working my last year as a principal, and still didn't know what I wanted to do "for real." So I applied to graduate school. (That's what we do, right? Get more education, because another degree, a different certificate—in my case, a doctorate—will solve all our problems. Riiight.)

I applied to only one program—at Harvard—and got in. The day I got my acceptance letter, I had a goal. I needed to pay off all my credit card debt and build my savings so when I walked out of my school building for the last time, I would have a little cushion to move to Cambridge, Massachusetts. I decided to use all my remaining paid time off to consult. Specifically, to offer full days of PD. So, for those of you saying you can't generate revenue in your business because of your 9-to-5, take note. How much does your job pay you to work for a day, and how much would you make if you used that day for consulting instead? In my case, my principal salary broke down to $191 a day. So, taking a $2,000 or $5,000 contract for that same day was a no-brainer. I got to work, built my cushion, and moved to Cambridge.

Jumping forward to 2019, I was now a full-time doctoral student.

In 2019, my business made $62,000 in revenue—nearly as much as my salary back in Charlotte. But because I was in school Monday through Friday, I couldn't offer professional development on weekdays anymore. So I pivoted once again, moving to one-on-one coaching and PD on weekends only. The meta moment here is that I chose a business model that worked with my life and my own goals. At the time, I was busy on weekdays, and the goal was more money. So I was working, studying, or attending class nearly every day. Again, notice—if the reason you can't work on your business is a day job, or school, or a commitment during normal working hours, it's possible to find a way to earn money and offer your services that works for you.

The lesson for me in 2019 and now for you: There's always another option.

A year later in 2020, my business was now generating $147,000 a year. I kept growing during lockdown. I had my first six-figure year despite being surrounded by people saying that it was impossible to do anything during COVID. What happened to me is proof that what you think determines your reality. The 2020–2021 academic school year was also the last year of my doctoral program at Harvard, which required a residency. I worked with a partner organization and wrote my dissertation about a research project I led. Unfortunately, what could have turned into a job or at least a fruitful relationship became yet another meta moment. I experienced countless microaggressions from my male supervisor that made it clear to me that I could not expect safety in systems that weren't designed for me.

Luckily, I had avoided this kind of situation for most of my leadership career, partly because I worked for some great bosses who were Black women who made it a point to professionally protect me. But here I was, a Harvard-educated Black woman with a soon-to-be *Dr.* in front of her name, and I was still labeled "aggressive and resistant." It made me realize that the only place I could guarantee my safety was in my own business. But I still had bills to pay.

So, I set a new goal, and you can copy it if you would like.

I want to make so much money in my business that taking a job would cause me to LOSE money.

Because to me, at that point, the math would be mathin', and even my overthinking, overanalytical brain couldn't talk me out of my heart's desire.

In April 2021, I defended my dissertation and made $63,000 consulting in that month alone. So, imagine my thoughts when receiving job offers for $120,000—annually. And, y'all, that's when I became really dangerous. I knew then that I had the power to generate whatever I needed. I looked for grants and was blessed to receive one for six figures that allowed me to pause, rest, and rebuild the foundation of my business. I decided to sell almost everything I owned, put what I wanted to keep in storage, and became a digital nomad for six months, traveling all around the world while growing my business. I went to St. Lucia, Mexico City, Hawaii, Los Angeles . . . another meta moment, because I know you may have that kind of travel or lifestyle on your bucket list—and I'm telling you that you can have it.

By the end of 2021, my business made over $500,000, and I paused again.

I wanted to keep growing, so the next step I took was hiring. I wanted to generate a million dollars in 2022, and to do that, I had to duplicate myself. I had already hired a full-time executive assistant, so next I hired coaches to help me with client delivery and an operations coordinator to help me grow the systems of the business. I upgraded my services with my bookkeeper and accountant, and I hired an attorney on retainer. I got ready to stay ready (more on that in Chapter 10). I made my million-dollar revenue goal in 2022 and every year since. Seven figures is now my new floor.

My next goal is eight figures—but I'm writing this in 2025. What I want you to recognize is how I went from side hustle to multimillion-dollar company in less than eight years.

As I'm writing this book in 2025, I employ five fellow Black women and, through my coaching and consulting, help hundreds of educators to create their own businesses and engineer their own paths to freedom. I'll be the first to admit that these are not normal results, because I'm not normal. But neither are you. That's my million-dollar story. But let's switch it up and talk about yours.

In this book, you will learn how to build a business from $0 to $250,000. Throughout these chapters, I'm going to ask you to map yourself onto my journey, and to keep doing so throughout this book. And, because we're all educators here, I'm going to apply pedagogy and cite my sources to back up what I say. What I want you to know is that the reason I've made the initial goal in this book $250,000 is because you gotta start with six figures to get to seven. However, I don't expect you to plan for a quarter million. Instead, we are backwards planning from seven figures. Because the *real* goal is for you to become a 7-Figure Educator, which I define as an education consulting business with annual revenue over a million dollars.

Throughout this book, I'm going to expose you to seven-figure conversations so that you can run the play all the way through. I'm sharing the blueprint of how I created my own success, giving you step-by-step instructions that will guide your way.

A note about terminology

I believe all oppression is connected. That said, in this book I have intentionally chosen to be specific regarding the use of **Black**, **BIPOC**, and *people of color*. To me, these are not mix-and-match terms. In short, when I mean Black, I say Black. When I mean BIPOC, I say BIPOC. And when I want to mean all people of color, I say people of color.

And, while this book has an intentional lens on the experiences of communities of color, I welcome all educators committed to equity and justice to this book, to our greater community of education consultants, and to all the programs I offer. Because every educator deserves to become a millionaire.

In Part I, *Clarify*, we'll work on getting your mind right. Chapter 1 is about understanding how the systems and society we exist in cloud our vision and make us doubt our own abilities. But I've met too many imposters in my time to believe I am one. (And I bet you have too.) By the end of the very first chapter, you'll understand what has held you back and how to change that 'ish. In Chapter 2, I'm going to help you dream bigger. I'll show you how to create a vision that supports the version of you who runs a seven-figure business:

who you need to become and even what you need to believe. In Chapter 3, I'll help you narrow your focus to solving one problem with your business. Repeat after me the word of Jay-Z with a Dr. EJT twist: There are 99 problems, but we must pick *one*. Chapter 4 offers up all the cheat codes to content creation. Like educational standards in the classroom, creating a framework for your business gives us a playground for our ideas and minimizes how much time we spend wondering what to talk about or concentrate on. By the end of this section, you will know what problem your business is solving and will be able to talk about it without confusing your grandmama.

In Part II, we *Build*. Chapter 5 outlines nine different service models that can work within education consulting, and I'll also teach you how to set up your offers so that clients can self-select ways to work with you based on their needs and budgets. In Chapter 6, I'll share my unique approach to defining your ideal client that will make identifying future clients as easy and seamless as talking to your best friend. Chapter 7 is all about pricing and avoiding what I did, which is undercharging for years because of guilt, reluctance, and fear around talking money. I'll share my best advice on how to price your services by teaching you two different approaches (market based and value based) that will allow you to see your offers objectively and set the right price from the start. Once you know what you're offering and how much you're going to charge, you'll learn how to build a basic marketing and sales process in Chapter 8. (Spoiler alert: We'll talk about your money mindset in that chapter too.) By the end of Part II, you will have everything you need to get your first client. And probably more—because by this point in the book, you'll have everything you need to be generating four figures of revenue consistently, month after month.

At that point, it's time to execute on Part III, *Grow*. In Chapter 9 I'll share my approach to branding, which is different from what you may have seen and heard from other entrepreneurial gurus. I'll also show you how a lesson from 10th-grade English composition can help you tell a memorable tale about your business that will attract even more of the right people. And the final chapter will show you how to create systems in your business so that when—not if—you expand, your business can grow as easily as you do.

As educators, I know you want to see the research and the evidence that this system is going to work for you. That's why I've included a concept from education or a research citation (or both) in every single chapter as a sort of teacher's guide to what you'll be learning. Along with meta moments from my own journey, I will also share lots of real-life stories from my clients who are educator-entrepreneurs like us to show how things can be done. By the end of this book, you'll have the step-by-step blueprint, supported by research, facts, and real success stories to become a 7-Figure Educator.

Let's start with this mic drop.

You've done this before.

When I hosted my first big live event in 2022, I realized something really simple, but equally as profound. You might have already realized this yourself. Everything I was teaching, everything I had learned as an entrepreneur—I had done as an educator.

Created offers.

Built a brand.

Marketed and sold.

Hired people.

Managed a team.

I had already led a business . . . the only difference was that my "business" was a middle school. And before that, a classroom. Let this be another meta moment for you. *You've done this before.* You've done all sorts of hard, challenging, complex tasks. Obviously, I don't know you personally. But I bet you could make a list right now if you wanted to. Maybe you've run a classroom, grown kids two to three years in a year's time, bootstrapped an entire after-school program, rolled out a new curriculum across an entire district, coached a cohort of principals, turned around a school or district. Maybe you've done all this while still showing up as a parent, caregiver, partner, best friend, etc. As educators and as leaders, we know how to do so many things at once. Trust in the fact that those experiences matter to this journey, and that your past—no matter how dramatic, underprivileged, underresourced, underpaid, or simply unjust—is going to help you succeed.

To prove this point, I want to share a story that comes from an unlikely source: the NBA. I'm not really a sports person, so what little I know about basketball, I was taught in elementary school. My PE teacher taught me that when you shoot a basket, you should aim for that orange square on the backboard, not the hoop. But when you look at a particular pro baller's shot—you won't see him hitting that square. Instead, Kyrie Irving, a NBA player who has played for teams like the Cleveland Cavaliers, Boston Celtics, and Dallas Mavericks, has a very unique shooting style. That's because when he was growing up, the court in his neighborhood had a broken backboard. Where there was supposed to be an orange square, his backboard literally had a hole. So, our boy Kyrie found his own way. He learned how to shoot the ball with a spin so it would hit the corner of the backboard and go in the basket. As it turns out, his experience of growing up in an environment where the basketball court had a broken backboard is what made him wildly successful.

Little Kyrie could have said, "There are missing pieces on the backboard. I can't play."

But instead, he got creative. And that's what I have done, and what you have done, and what you will do.

Instead of focusing on what you don't have—focus on what you do.

In a lot of ways, as educators we have been dealt a broken backboard. The classrooms we've taught in, schools and districts we've led in were underresourced. Most of us have not been paid a fair, living wage. The neighborhood and family you grew up in probably didn't look like *The Cosby Show*.

But you're here anyway. With a bunch of receipts for the successes you have earned and your own meta moments where you found your own way. And, like Kyrie, you are uniquely positioned to succeed *because* of your past circumstances, not despite them. Because your past experiences, your résumé, your personal story have taught you and conditioned you to do something different. And that's what makes you special and sets you up to succeed.

All you need is the blueprint. Let's get started on your journey to becoming a 7-Figure Educator.

Clarify

You Are the 2%

Objective: You will understand what has actually held you back (Spoiler alert: it's not you)

I'm gonna say this with my whole chest.

I despise the concept of "imposter syndrome." I believe the concept of imposter syndrome normalizes feelings of inadequacy. Because when you're in a room that doesn't look like you and you feel like you don't belong, the typical response is, "Oh, I must have imposter syndrome."

How about there is something wrong with the MF'in room?

Everything you learned about imposter syndrome is a lie. Imposter syndrome puts the focus on how historically oppressed people need to change instead of interrogating the oppressive, exclusionary systems we find ourselves in. And yet self-diagnosed imposter syndrome is still the biggest thing holding you back from being a 7-Figure Educator. So, we gon' talk about the topic I despise so we can answer the question I get asked so often: "How do you overcome imposter syndrome?"

I can't tell you how many teachers I know who have used every ounce of their genius to achieve the impossible in their classrooms, only to feel like their absolute best is never enough or that they're not allowed to want more. I've heard hundreds of stories from Black educators and educators of color who run circles around their peers yet still think that they don't belong in competitive spaces, even though they eat 'em up every time and leave no crumbs.

In the early days of my educational consulting business, I thought I struggled with this imposter mentality too. I would question if I belonged, question my own decisions, and doubt my dream. I graduated undergrad a quarter early, made double-digit gains in student achievement every year as a high school math teacher, was named a New Teacher of the Year finalist for my district—one of the largest school districts in the country—was recognized as 30 Under 30 by the city, as principal led my school to be ranked in the top one percent of student growth in the state, and still . . . there was this script running through my head, telling me to ignore any evidence that I was a certified fierce, first-class badass.

Maybe you hear that script echoing in your thoughts too. Maybe it's telling you that what you do isn't special, so how can you be capable of something bold and audacious like starting your own consulting business? Because who's gonna pay *you*? Maybe it's claiming that you're somehow different, lesser, than the people you see whose businesses are thriving. Maybe it's saying that dream of financial freedom isn't meant for you. Well, let me hit you with the truth.

That script is raggedy . . . with a capital *R*. And that script may be currently in you, but it's not of you. Let me explain.

Something else is writing every line of your self-doubt. In his poem "How to Explain White Supremacy to a White Supremacist," poet and activist Kyle "Guante" Tran Myhre provides a powerful analogy for how to think of racism. Racism is not the shark, he says, but the water we all are swimming in. While you've been out in the world, being everything to everyone, you've been swimming in the water. You've internalized the water without realizing it, swimming in its lies since the day you entered this earth and then blaming yourself for not feeling worthy of success, praise, and respect.

Of course, that "water" is a powerful, centuries-old societal system that privileges white, heterosexual, cisgender, able-bodied, English-speaking, Christian men. One that was purposely designed to keep anyone who doesn't check all those boxes, aka badasses like me and you, away from the spotlight and living in the shadows. A system that wants you to give up before you even start.

With this framing, let me ask you this important question: If you're a Black educator or an educator of color navigating this system that wasn't created for you, are *you* the problem here? Or is the problem the system that has perpetuated a lack of belonging and financial suppression?

Remember when I said everything you've learned about imposter syndrome is a lie? I know it was spicy, but follow me here as I give you a little background on how the concept of imposter syndrome came to be. The term was introduced in 1978 by clinical psychologists Pauline Clance and Suzanne Imes. Based on a study they did on high-achieving professional women, imposter syndrome was defined as "an internal experience of intellectual phoniness." The women that Clance and Imes evaluated seemed to believe that no matter how much they accomplished, they were essentially tricking everyone. Somehow these bona fide badass ladies just couldn't accept the fact that they were deserving of what they flat-out earned.

As this study made waves and became popular in the mainstream, there were a lot of conversations about why women seemed to be victims of their own irrational insecurities. Everything from family dynamics and parenting styles to high-pressure workplaces and personality traits appeared to be part of the cause.

But over time, many scholars, particularly in the Black community, started giving the imposter syndrome theory some serious and well-deserved side-eye.

Why?

Well, here's the tea.

The results of the original study were skewed AF. Almost all the participants were basically carbon copies of each other—white and upper class. The lack of diversity in the subject group meant the historical and cultural contexts that impact Black people and people of color weren't taken into account at all. The influence of racism was completely absent from the data.

That means the open hostility and microaggressions that communities of color face, especially in predominantly white environments, weren't even a footnote in the research.

That means the hoops Black people have to jump through in order to be seen as human—much less exceptional—weren't even a blip on the radar.

The glaring absence of the Black experience in the foundation of the concept of imposter syndrome has extended to today. It's a theory that was never truly about us, but we somehow have come to embody it anyway.

So, I have another question for you to chew on: Is it possible that your imposter syndrome has been a coping mechanism all along?

In her book *Sisters of the Yam*, activist and writer bell hooks wrote that navigating white systems requires vigilant self-scrutiny and a willingness to place oneself in the mind-set of the oppressor to avoid punishment. hooks argues that when your focus is on avoiding punishment, you can't focus on self-affirmation. Think about it. Are you more likely to point out what you need to improve before you identify where you have exceeded the expectation? Do you turn criticism on yourself because it isn't safe for you to talk about a system that wants to dismiss and deject you? Have you been suppressing your feelings because you believe it gives you an edge, or maybe because you're trying to avoid being viewed as "aggressive"? Imposter syndrome is the way we as Black people and people of color have adopted the mindset of the oppressor in order to avoid punishment. We've had to call out our own faults before the system calls them out for us. We've had to operate with a level of hyperawareness, to assess how best to conform, in order to stay safe in rooms that weren't intended for us.

Throughout this chapter, I want you to think deeply on this, because you must reframe imposter syndrome in order to clap back against it—so you can move toward a path of self-affirmation with less fear and insecurity. Creating a new paradigm where you know deep in your bones how brilliant you are will guide you toward your goals with a sense of purpose and confidence. Changing your inner dialogue from "Wealth and success isn't attainable for me" to "I come from a lineage of sacrifice and perseverance, and wealth and success are ways I honor my ancestors and just an ounce of the reparations I am owed." This is the shift that will allow you to launch an educational consulting business that will make an impact on your community. And receive a significant glow-up in the process too.

But first, you gotta take out any garbage beliefs you might have about you and your quest for a bountiful, abundant life.

You can't become the 7-Figure Educator you are meant to be when your mind is cluttered with thoughts and behaviors that don't serve you.

You can't experience financial freedom if you don't believe that wealth, ease, and prosperity are your birthright.

So, in order to shed imposter syndrome and whatever other garbage beliefs you've got, you have to recognize that you've been swimming in the water, and that has shaped how you view the world. In order to change your beliefs, you first have to *see* them. You have to see what I call "the optics of oppression." When I say optics, I mean the way in which you view the world. Oppression clouds your view, shifts your beliefs, and alters your perspective. And if you think the optics of oppression haven't impacted you, remember you have been swimming in the water; we all have. So it's not IF you're impacted by the optics of oppression, but rather how.

Before we dive into the details of how, let me define what the word *oppression* means in this context. Oppression is the combination of prejudice and institutional power that creates a system that discriminates against some groups (often called *target groups*) and benefits other groups (often called *dominant groups*). If you identify as a person of color, your economic mobility (rightfully) challenges the existing power structures. That challenge might feel confronting and uncomfortable at times, but it's to be expected as you step into uncharted territory.

Also, I'd like to offer up this disclaimer. I've been the Black woman in those DEI trainings who left feeling more angry than educated. My goal in sharing this framework isn't to discourage you or to make you feel any kind of way (including but not limited to guilty, angry, shameful, mournful, or more oppressed). My goal is to help you see the "water" you've internalized that is hurting you and your potential business before you can even get it off the ground.

Once you do that, you can finally own your future.

So, grab your favorite after–5 P.M. beverage, find a comfortable place to sit, and let's get into it.

Lens #1—Mountains

The first way that optics of oppression shows up is how it influences how you see mountains. Not real mountains, but figurative ones. Your challenges. Your obstacles. Whatever stands in the way between where you are now and where you want to be. The way you see those mountains and whether you believe you can move them is often influenced by the insidious nature of oppression.

Let's test this theory out for a minute.

What thoughts pop into your mind after reading these statistics?

- Only 9 percent of businesses generate $1,000,000+ in annual revenue.

- Only 2 percent of women-owned businesses cross the seven-figure mark.

That means 90 percent of businesses never make a milly. And, chile, we ain't even cut these numbers by race.

Did you assume that you're not going to be part of those statistical successes right from the jump?

Did you hear a little voice in your head say something like, *Nine as in one less than ten? Two as in one, two? Shit, I'm never going to get there.*

Maybe you started to consider how much you currently make. Let's say your salary is $50,000. At that rate, you'd have to work 20 years before making a million dollars, and now we are talking making that much in one year? You might be thinking, *Yes, that's definitely a mountain.*

If any of this rang true, the optics of oppression has you interpreting that information as a barrier that excludes you.

You see it as a mountain that is virtually impassible, a blockage that you'll never be able to move.

But the optics of oppression is a mental game of smoke and mirrors. It's playing with you. It wants you to believe that you're not special, talented, or badass enough to climb that mountain and put your stake at the top—or blow a hole right through it. It encourages you to hold yourself back and tell yourself you're going to fail before you even begin.

Making a million dollars in a year used to feel far-fetched to me too. Then one day I had an experience, a kind of aha moment—the kind of aha that makes oppression real nervous. I was going live on social media with a friend of mine who had asked me to talk about my growing business. They started with reading my bio, which states that I received a doctorate degree from Harvard.

They said, *"Harvard, wow!* That's a hard school to get into. What is their acceptance rate? Like *2 percent?"*

That's when it hit me.

Holy shit, I am the 2%. I've BEEN the 2%.

I got accepted to Harvard at 31. I became a school principal at 28. I became an assistant principal at 25. I graduated early from college.

And if we wanted to take it all the way back to high school, I passed the AP Calculus test with flying colors.

That's a lot of 2% behavior!

Oppression will have you focusing on the mountain and doubting your abilities.

But the reframe I want to offer—the lens cleaner, if you will—is that you, too, have *been* the 2%.

If you have an advanced degree—a master's or a doctorate—you are the 2%.

If you are a Black male educator, you are the 2%.

If you've been "the only" in a room—the only woman, the only Black male, the only Latina, etc.—you're the 2%.

Women who look like me and maybe you—i.e., Black women—make up only 2% of tenured professors, 2% of doctors, 2% of political candidates . . . I could go on.

It is safe to assume that launching and leading a business that makes a million dollars in annual revenue will not be your first time succeeding where others can't, won't, or don't. Oppression is trying to make you believe that you can't go from hustling and struggling as an educator to bringing in 20 times your current salary with confidence and conviction. It's trying to rob you of your successful track record—in the classroom, in the schoolhouse, in your district, and anywhere else. It keeps people who look like you out of positions of power and influence so that you don't see many reflections of yourself.

Because if you did, you would see the mountains in front of you as no match for your energy, ingenuity, and courage.

You would know that you don't just climb mountains, you *move* them.

Lens #2—Overworking

The second way that oppression goes on the attack is by convincing you that you need to do *more* in order to succeed—and that overworking is the only way to reach your goals. I'm going to break down why in Chapter 9, but for now, I'm sure you would agree that a lot of this comes from our upbringing. Most marginalized folks were raised to believe that we need to work twice as hard to get half the opportunities of our affluent white peers. Our well-intentioned parents taught us to always be doing the most so we could have more choices and chances to level up. Oppression has our whole community in a choke hold, believing that rippin' and runnin' is normal. That if we aren't breaking our backs, we're lazy, we aren't doing enough, and we're a bad representation of our community (lawd, talk about extreme!). The water of oppression sets us up for burnout, people pleasing, perfectionism, and a total lack of boundaries.

When you move into your business believing that you have to work twice as hard, you will lose money, point blank.

We've normalized overworking to the point that when we do become our own bosses, we often cling to our old, conventional ways. I did this myself when I started my business. There I was, on my own with no time sheet to turn in, but still working 9-to-5, keeping an eye on the clock whenever I took a break. If you catch yourself counting hours, responding to e-mails on weekends, or don't feel like yourself without a never-ending to-do list, you have also normalized overworking.

The good news is that when you've been socialized to believe that you have to work twice as hard, your 50 percent is good enough. Your 50 percent is actually most of the world's 100 percent.

Let me give you an example of what the shift from overworking to embracing your 50 percent could look like. You probably think you need a website and a fancy logo in order to start your business. That website is going to take weeks, or even months, to build, because you need to design it and write and format the copy on each page. You need to link to your social media accounts and determine how you want people to contact you. And then it's, "Oh, wait, I don't have any headshots!" Now you're booking a whole-ass photoshoot after you research the best photographers near you. While all this is going on, you've received no revenue for your business. The website became a must-do because you believed that what you had to start with wasn't enough.

This is "you have to work twice as hard" at work.

The truth is, you don't need much to get your business off the ground. In fact, your first six-figure contracts are already waiting for you in your network. Meet your new clients: the first principal you worked for, a former co-worker who is now in charge of professional development, a fraternity brother or sorority sister who runs the Curriculum & Instruction department for their district. None of them need a website to know who you are and what you bring to the table, because they already know you! You just need to make the contact: Simply send an e-mail, pick up the phone, or text them that you are now the CEO of your own business.

To put this in academic terms: Your C is somebody else's A+.

Knowing that you're being graded on a curve, you can relax, relate, and release the idea that doing literally all the things is the only way to achieve.

And when the world doesn't end, relax a bit more.

Remember: You're not an imposter. You're the 2%. You don't have to work yourself to the bone to get what you righteously deserve.

Lens #3—You Are Not Normal

When I started to really grow my business, people who had known me for years all of a sudden started telling me that I'd changed. Me being on social media talking about money and wealth made some folks around me uncomfortable. But to be honest, I didn't feel like I had changed all that much. Then I realized something: The people saying I had changed were the same people who applauded me when I was over-worked and underpaid.

That living-paycheck-to-paycheck, tolerant, I'll-make-do person is gone and had to go, because she could not and would not run an eight-figure business, and that's who I'm becoming. So, yes, I did change.

What this change taught me is that I'm not normal—and neither are you.

Oppression has you thinking that you're ordinary. Because if you see yourself as the unicorn you are, then you're likely to become a disrupter of the status quo, and oppression can't have that.

But you're part of the 2%, remember? That means you have to embrace being an outlier. That means you have to ready yourself for 98 percent of people misunderstanding your vision, your beliefs, and your actions.

If that makes you feel a little nervous, I get it. You're an educator. Your life's work has been about helping your students to understand the content you teach and the world around them. The thought of not being understood could be sending you sideways.

It's okay. Discomfort doesn't have to mean that something bad is happening. In fact, disruption precedes transformation. You just have to give yourself some space to grow and change.

Here's something else to keep in mind. When I say we're not normal, I am not saying we are "better than." There's no judgment here for other folks who want different things. But knowing that you're not the norm allows you to push back on the optics of oppression that will say that if you are going to move like a millionaire, you must move in silence, because too many people would become uncomfortable.

Certain people can't handle the way I talk about money.

Certain people can't handle the way I spend what I earn.

Hell, some people can't handle the fact that I don't like to drive and choose not to own a car. Black car me, please.

What they think doesn't matter.

You're the 2%—which means you don't need anyone's permission to play by whatever rules you want. I promise you that your life opens up so much when you decide to embrace being different and stop apologizing for it.

Let me give you an example from my own life.

When I crossed the seven-figure mark for the first time, managing my business and my personal life became *a lot* to handle. I would order packages to my Amazon locker, and they would end up getting returned because I would forget to pick them up. I was using a meal-prep service and I kept missing the Friday 5 P.M. deadline to order my meals for the week. And let's not even talk about the laundry that was piling up all around the house. I told myself that I should be able to handle these things because they were "little" and not a big deal.

Then I had a game-changing conversation with my therapist. I admitted that while I was killing it in my business, my personal life was a hot mess express.

She said something so simple: "It sounds like you need some help."

My response was, "But these are normal things I should be able to do!"

Then like a book she read me and said, "That's something Erica five years ago might have been able to handle. But these are not normal times. You are running a million-dollar business now. It's okay to hire someone to help manage your personal life, just like how you would hire help for your business."

Her words set me free. I had been holding on to a "normal" 98 percent life filled with laundry, washing dishes, and picking up packages when I needed to focus on securing $50,000 contracts.

Was this breaking the majority rule? Maybe.

But I'm not normal. I do what makes sense for me.

So I hired a personal assistant who never missed a delivery, set up a laundry service for me, and ordered my meals every Friday by 5 P.M.

Ninety-eight percent of folks may not understand why I pay someone to pick up my packages, and that's okay.

I'm used to it now. And soon you will be too.

Lens #4—Environment

The fourth way that the optics of oppression manifests is in our environment. When I teach the idea of interrogating your environment in my workshops, most folks immediately assume that I mean the people who make up our inner circles. The friends, family, and co-workers who doubt or complain, or whose presence affects us on a daily basis. (If that happens for you—you've got some relationships to review.)

However, our environment is expansive. It's made up of everything we encounter on a daily basis. The city and neighborhood you live in, where you work, the places you spend the most time in, the clothes you wear, how you treat your body, what you say no or yes to.

All these things are a reflection of your expectations and what you are willing to accept.

Often, because the environment we grew up in, or at some point got used to, is all we know, we learn to unconsciously live with low expectations. I say this kindly and with a lot of understanding, but teachers, especially, have become accustomed to existing in a broke, scarce mindset. And who can blame us, given the working conditions we're used to?

That's kind of the point. In order for oppression to be successful, you have to believe there are not enough resources to go around. If there's not enough, you'll believe that it doesn't make sense to try to get more than what you have. Thinking you don't or will never have enough also keeps you feeling small and stuck in survival mode. It will have you focused on getting through each day rather than looking ahead and creating a vision of the abundant environment you want for yourself.

Which is why you need to shed the things in your life that have you thinking and feeling less than and lacking. For instance, I used to sleep in my old college T-shirts. Although I loved wearing them to bed because they were familiar, I wore those when I made $33,000 a year as a high school math teacher. I was going to bed every night wrapped in fabric from a time when I couldn't afford much. But when I became an educational consultant and started to quote clients a price that used to be my old salary, I wanted my environment to reflect where I was going, not where I was before. If I wanted to charge $33K to a single client, I couldn't sleep in the energy of a time when I was making $33K a year. So one of the first things I did when I had disposable income was buy myself a nice pair of cotton pajamas and a silk robe. When I went to bed, I felt so much more secure and confident.

I started making other changes in my environment that I felt would help channel the energy of my aspirations. Every November I block off a whole week to conduct my annual planning for the following year. Instead of conducting that business at home, I intentionally do this work somewhere that represents the bold leveling-up plan I always have for next year. I love my house, but it's a reflection of my current reality and routines. My annual planning is focused on change and evolution, so I always pick a new destination that I want to explore. And I book a suite because I want a space big enough to hold the vision I will be cooking up.

So far, my favorite places to strategize have been a five-star hotel in Las Vegas and the Four Seasons in Jackson Hole,

Wyoming, but wherever I choose to go, I know that I belong there. Just like you, I am part of the 2% and my environment reflects that. We hold the keys to every single door we care to unlock and have earned a seat at any table we wanna roll up on.

Lens #5—Your Yes

The final way the optics of oppression affects you is in how it keeps you from recognizing that you have the power to decide the terms of your own life. You can choose what you say yes and no to every day of the week, and twice on Sundays. Oppression has you feeling like your decisive power is an external thing that you have to search for instead of something you need to awaken within yourself.

You've said yes to things because you didn't have the option to say no—you've had bills to pay and mouths to feed, and that doesn't stop being true when you start your own business. In the beginning, you might have to say yes to everything. But as your business grows and develops—and as *you* grow and develop—you get to operate from a place of desire and ambition instead of just survival. You can afford to be picky, choosy, and particular.

Here's a great example. In any given week, I get two or three requests from educators asking to connect. Most are aspiring business owners who are wondering how to make the leap from their 9-to-5. The DM usually ends with something like, "I'd love to schedule some time to talk with you." Early on in my business, I said yes to these requests. I had the time, I wanted to know more about what educators were going through (because y'all are my ideal clients), and I truly wanted to be helpful. But today my answer is no. I still want to be helpful, but I have had to shift from offering my time one-on-one to offering content that is available one-to-many.

I have free content available online right now that could likely answer any questions sooner than I could make time on my calendar. And, frankly, spending time on individual calls causes me to lose money because it takes me away from my business.

Your yeses are going to change throughout your journey and ultimately your life.

Once you embrace the full power of saying no to what doesn't meet you where you are or align with where you are going, you'll see why oppression was trying to keep you from that power for as long as possible. Part of growth as a business owner is understanding how the power of our answers affects our everyday lives and becoming really intentional about your yes. You may have visions of millions, of a seven-figure business, but if you're still saying yes to four-figure opportunities (or giving away for free what people will pay for), you're not going to get there. That's why to change, ascend, and reach your goals, you need to redefine what an enthusiastic yes looks like.

THE HIDDEN IMPACT OF MOUNTAINS

You may have noticed a hidden message in this chapter about oppression. Here it is, in black and white:

Mountains	Environment
Overworking	Your Yes
Normality	

Yep. Your relationship with and choices around money—earning it, keeping it, spending it, saving it, investing it, donating it—are heavily influenced by the optics of oppression.

Most of us don't even realize how deep the impact goes, because it's all we know, right?

While I don't believe that money can solve all your problems (it solves a lot) or that it speaks to the quality of your character, it is a big part of how we achieve our liberty and extend our legacy. We all were called to the teaching profession for different reasons, and none of them were likely dollar signs. But building your own business and pursuing opportunities that will broaden your horizons and allow you to flourish the way you were meant to isn't selling out or turning your back on a community you've come to love.

Oppression feeds on your guilt. Its power over you grows whenever you equate advocating for yourself and desiring more with being selfish and abandoning your values. Oppression functions best when you sacrifice your hopes and dreams. It cheers as it traps you in a confusing cycle where you can't tell up from down, because then you think you're helpless. Except you're not helpless. None of us 2%-ers are. When you're fully aware of how the optics of oppression mess with you, I promise you can see them for the illusions they are and do whatever the hell you please.

Here's a great analogy I use to get this point across to my clients.

At the 2020 Olympics in Tokyo, Simone Biles removed herself from the competition because she was experiencing a phenomenon called the Twisties. This mental block can create a body-mind disconnect for gymnasts, causing them to lose their sense of location midair while performing flips and twists. It's scary and dangerous because the gymnast, for even the briefest moment, has no sense of control over their movement and position in space. They might not even recognize what element they're performing—is it the balance beam, the uneven bars, floor exercise?

The optics of oppression can do the same thing to your sense of direction and perception of your place in the world. They distort everything in your view—whether it's your past, your present, or your potential future.

However, what I want you to remember about Simone's story is not that she had the Twisties—because that's not her damn fault, right?—it's the choices she made in the face of them.

2%-type choices.

Instead of putting her physical safety at risk, she withdrew from the competition. Which is a MAJOR flex. Simone chose to protect herself rather than listen to the opinions of millions of other people who claimed she'd be letting her country down if she stepped aside. She chose her peace of mind when reporters questioned her decision to cheer her teammates on from the sidelines and focus on her recovery.

She said yes to herself.

She was unbothered by the pressure being put on her, because she didn't just belong in the arena—the arena belonged TO HER.

Simone Biles went on to make the biggest comeback in sports history, becoming the first gymnast to win eight United States all-around titles at the next Olympics, and the oldest one to do so.

You, too, are going to experience entrepreneurial Twisties. Oppression will attempt to cloud your perspective and your judgment. Some form of imposter syndrome will reappear at inconvenient times and places, causing you to doubt yourself and what you deserve. But once you recognize those lies for what they are, all you need are the tools to help you pave the way for your gold-medal moment—and a support system that is going to cheer for your success.

This book is your tool kit, and I am your teammate rooting for you like crazy.

So, let's get going.

CHAPTER 1 REFLECTION QUESTIONS

1. What mountains have you been overestimating? How have you been underestimating your ability to move them?

2. What does overworking look like for you? Be specific. You have to name it in order to change it.

3. How are you not normal? How have you tried to fit in even though you are exceptional?

4. How will your environment need to shift in order to fully step into your identity as a 7-Figure Educator?

5. What have you been giving your yes to that actually deserves your no?

ACTION STEPS

Identify times in your professional and personal experience when you've been the 2%. Think holistically. Consider your professional degrees, times when you were "the only," as well as your "twice as good" accomplishments.

7-FIGURE EDUCATOR RESOURCES

Visit **www.7febook.com/resources** to:

- Watch Episode 35: "The Woes of Imposter Syndrome (and How to Beat it!)" of the *7-Figure Educator* podcast to further unlearn your relationship with imposter syndrome

Your Freedom Formula

Objective: Know how to dream bigger and set initial goals

In a world that excludes people who look like you and me, dreaming is a revolutionary act. Dreaming is a gateway from just surviving. Dreaming is a self-honor practice that allows you to see beyond your current reality. Dreaming acknowledges your power to create what doesn't yet exist. As novelist and fellow educator Toni Morrison said, "As you enter positions of trust and power, dream a little before you think."

This chapter is going to get you dreaming. Bigger than you might ever have before.

So: What does it mean to dream big?

We need to answer that question before we go any further. Because if you continue to think small, nothing in this book will work for you. (Or at least, it won't work as well as it could.) When I teach in person what I'm about to share, I always notice a few people in the audience with a skeptical look. Those folks think something like, *That might have worked for her, but it won't for me because of X, Y, Z.*

I call out the skepticism, but I don't judge it. Educators are used to working in school systems that have a set salary schedule based on your level of education and years of experience. There's absolutely no room for negotiation or even increases based on merit and performance. As a result, so many educators base their dreams of what's possible on the same type of salary schedule. According to the National Education Association (NEA), the average salary for a teacher in the U.S. in 2025 is $62,714. (My salary as a teacher in 2017 was $33,000.) But the average yearly cost of living per household is $61,334. That leaves the average educator with $1,380 "extra" *per year* after paying for housing, food, transportation, utilities, and health care.

It's easy to see why you might be dreaming small based on that data. Your dreams have been limited to your salary schedule. You might be thinking, *Well, I make more than that*—and I hear you. But dreaming big first requires you to "see" the way the system has conditioned you to dream small. Regardless of how much you're earning, even if it's six figures, you could be making that amount faster . . . because you could be making six figures in a day. I know, because I've done it.

Let me drop this truth: **There is no difference between me and you.**

And if you think there is, that's a mindset issue.

Let's wind the clock back. There was a time when I thought I couldn't make more money. When I tried to budget my way to freedom. Let me remind you how this all started. Running out of gas on the side of the road. A single day of professional development for $1,600.

Here's how it's going now (at least as I'm writing this in the summer of 2025): seven figures in annual revenue every single year since 2022. How it's going is being able to hire my sister to work for my company, allowing her to quit her

$15-an-hour job. How it's going is becoming a real estate investor with five properties I can go to and enjoy whenever I want. How it's going is managing a team of 21, including 4 employees. How it's going is landing a six-figure deal with a dream publisher.

That was all possible—once I realized I could dream bigger than before.

I'm sharing that with you again so you see the shift.

Going from literally stranded on the side of the road to flying first class between homes I own in four different cities. All because of the shifts I made, internally and externally.

I'll say it again. There's no difference between me and you.

Therefore—and shoutout to the math educators who *know* this is the transitive property in action—if it's possible for me, then it's possible for you. Throughout this book, I'm going to talk about the hidden curriculum of entrepreneurship. Here's our first lesson in that curriculum.

Your beliefs about yourself and what's possible determine what's possible.

Back in the day when I was struggling financially, that version of me didn't believe I could have a seven-figure business. She was focused on surviving. She wanted to pay her bills. She couldn't see past my next paycheck. I was down so bad, I literally couldn't put enough gas in my car without a loan.

Contrast that with the version of me attending the London Business School with 75 fellow entrepreneurs who were preparing to scale their businesses. I had to make multiple shifts in my thinking to even be invited into that room—because the requirement for participation in the course was having more than a million dollars in annual revenue.

My point is, you have to change your thinking in order to change your life. You can't do the same things and expect your business to grow. Instead, you shift what you believe is possible so that you *can* dream bigger. So that you *can* start to implement the strategies, the behaviors, the thinking that will lead to your unique seven-figure vision.

Helping you to dream bigger is what this chapter is about. I'm going to start by helping you understand the mindsets that keep educators like you and me small. I'll identify three archetypical identities that hold us back, as well as the singular shift we can make to bring us back to what we were meant to be the whole damn time. I'll offer a path to creating intergenerational wealth. And then it's time to have fun.

By the end of this chapter, you will have identified and defined two strategic goals:

- Your Freedom Number, which will allow your business to replace your salary (so you can leave your job if you want) and set yourself up for financial stability and success.

- Your Abundance Number, which is the amount of money you need to fund your dream lifestyle (because that IS possible, no matter how bougie or unattainable you feel it may be).

THE THREE IDENTITIES THAT KEEP YOU PLAYING SMALL

Every Thanksgiving, I watch *The Wiz*. It's always been one of my favorite movies, but after I hit a million dollars in my business for the first time, it hit different. I noticed details I hadn't before, like the fact that Dorothy, played by Diana Ross, is a teacher who has just been reassigned to high school. Chile, no wonder she was struggling to believe in herself getting back home!

What really struck me is that the three characters Dorothy traveled through Oz with—Scarecrow, Tinman, and the cowardly Lion—are representations of the mindsets that were holding Dorothy back from what she truly and deeply wanted. And these, as it turns out, are the same mindsets I see in educators like yourself who may be thinking and dreaming too small.

You forget who you are

In *The Wiz,* Scarecrow, played by the iconic Michael Jackson, travels with Dorothy because he wants to ask the Wiz for a brain. He doubts his own ability. The only solo song Michael has during the entire movie is literally titled "You Can't Win." The lyrics say over and over again that the odds are stacked against him, that nothing ever changes, and that he can't do anything to improve his circumstances. To be honest, this used to be my favorite song in the movie because *hello, it's Michael Jackson,* until I realized what the lyrics actually said. He's saying, I'm in over my head. I will inevitably fail. Nothing is ever going to change. It's very woe-is-me.

But what I want you to recognize is that none of those statements are real or true. Instead, as proven throughout the course of the movie, the only thing holding Scarecrow back *is* those beliefs. I know the educators I work with are operating from a Scarecrow mindset when they forget or discount what they've accomplished or claim to have no power to change their circumstances. And especially when they say they can't win. Now, someone might not say those exact words, but the mindset always reveals itself. I've heard educators who have amazing accomplishments, like growing their students' reading levels at least two years within a year's time, wonder out loud whether anyone would pay them. (Ummmmm, hell yes.) Or who openly tell me they don't know anyone to pitch their services to after working in education for 25 years. (Trust me, you know plenty of people.)

When deep self-doubt comes up or you believe you have zero agency, Scarecrow is present for you. The big lesson in *The Wiz* is that even though Scarecrow assumes he is deficient and therefore doesn't have much to contribute, the opposite is true. As it turns out, the only reason that he—and you—can't win or don't win is because you're thinking and dreaming too small.

You forget your purpose

Working in education trains us to say yes and to do things even when we don't want to. You might love the kids in your school, but you dread getting assigned to field trips. But as an educator, when you get that assignment, there's no choice. On the field trip you go. Even when we become entrepreneurs who presumably have as much freedom as we want, that lack of control that we're used to as educators shows up. In the hours you work, in the prices you set, in the offers you make, and maybe even in the type of work you do. At a psychological level, this makes sense. It's basic conditioning. When you've been trained to settle, it's easy to continue settling. When you've been taught to play it safe, it's easy to become complacent when what you have seems like enough.

What I see among the educators I work with, and have experienced myself, is a sort of emotional numbness. Because we haven't had agency, sometimes for our entire careers, we're not used to being able to choose for ourselves based on our emotions and intuition. As educators, and especially as educators of color, it can feel challenging to make decisions based primarily on our own desires. Putting ourselves first can feel scary, especially when we're faced with figuring out what we really want—both from the business we're creating and from life itself.

In *The Wiz*, Tinman, played by legendary Nipsey Russell, wanted to ask for a heart because he wanted to feel.

When I hear an educator say that their 9-to-5 or their family obligations prevent them from finding the time for their business or their desires, I know Tinman is present. I know that you wouldn't be putting everybody else first if you were in touch with your purpose. Purpose allows us to know, really deeply on a spiritual level, why the way we show up matters. Purpose paints the picture of the freedom that is connected to the growth of our businesses—freedom of the clients we serve but also freedom for our families, the community, the society, the world that we all exist in.

When you understand what your calling is. When you understand why God designed you the exact way you are. When you understand the impact that saying yes to your business can have—there's zero question what your priorities are. You don't waffle over what your offers are going to be or hesitate over going all in. You know that your business is going to work, that entrepreneurship is the right choice, so you make time because your business supports your purpose, and your purpose cultivates your freedom. Like Tinman, in the end your heart and your emotion fuels you.

When you're in touch with your purpose, reasons why you can't become excuses, and no excuse in the world is going to stop you.

You let fear win

The cowardly Lion, played by Broadway star Ted Ross, wanted to ask the Wiz for courage. You might hesitate when you know it's time to raise your prices. Or you might worry what people at your job will think when you start your side hustle or when you quit. Or you might feel scared to hire help even though your business is bursting at the seams. You might be basing your decision-making on fear, opting for safety and security rather than possibility, potential, and abundance.

Here's a great example. When I did a tour stop in New York, an educator told me that she didn't want to leave her job until she was fully covered for retirement. What was going on in that educator's mind was the exact opposite of how seven- and eight-figure entrepreneurs think. For that educator, their priority was putting money away for the future over a long period of time. Let's do some math.

In New York City, new teachers with a bachelor's degree earn ~$75,000 annually and are required to contribute ~4 percent of that salary to retirement with New York State, adding ~10 percent as an employer contribution. That means every teacher earning $75,000 adds at least $10,500 to their account annually. Given that the stock market has an annualized return of 14.2 percent every five years and teachers in New York get an average 3.25 percent salary increase annually as well, that educator would end up with approximately $3 million in her investment accounts when she retires after 25 years.

Or she could just build a business that makes $3 million a year.

The shift is from fear—

I don't want to lose that money.

As long as I work at this school, my contributions are matched.

I have to wait until my benefits vest.

I need to know that I'll be okay in retirement.

—to abundance, because you know that your business is going to generate enough. Sitting with seven- and eight-figure entrepreneurs at the London Business School, retirement was talked about only in terms of the benefits we could offer to attract great employees. Because *our* retirement was never even in question.

FINDING YOUR SILVER RUBY SLIPPERS

Like Glinda the Good, the witch played by the legendary Lena Horne, reminded Dorothy in *The Wiz*, we all have the power to bring ourselves back home. (Just call me your Glinda!) For me, there were a series of little moments that, looking back, were whispers to dream bigger. Getting my first contract to deliver a day of PD for $1,600. That moment blew my mind because it was the first time I realized I could control my money. And, therefore, that money didn't control me. Remember that good ole salary schedule I talked about? The one you didn't get to negotiate and your performance, no matter how exceptional, didn't really affect? Contrast that with entrepreneurship, where there is no chart, no limit.

The first time I got a consulting gig, the money I made was the same amount as a week's pay as a principal. The next contract paid off all my credit card debt. After that, I was able to use every single contract I got to save money, and later, to attend Harvard. Even when I was earning my doctorate, when my colleagues and classmates were talking about having to take underpaid teaching fellow positions to bring in more income, I was good. I had my business, and I had contracts coming in. Instead of fighting over the few available work-study spots that paid only $30 per hour, I was signing $10,000 contracts or $20,000 contracts to do PD.

Every single time I signed a contract, it was a Dorothy moment. I took another step home. My Dorothy moments have helped me cast off the identities that kept me playing small, helped me get clear on my purpose, and helped me move past fear. And to this day, I'm still doing that. Over and over and over again. You will too.

As I'm writing this, I have a goal to buy a commercial building. When I work with my first commercial lender to help me, when I make an offer, when I get the keys, and when I host my first event in my own building . . . I'll unlock more Dorothy moments. While our goals might be different, every step I take and every step you take will bring us both closer to home and closer to who we're meant to be.

But there's something else I want you to recognize and get familiar with.

The core lesson of *The Wiz* is that your beliefs influence your thoughts, and your thoughts influence your actions. Cognitive brain science has overwhelmingly proven this to be true. When you are hesitating to take action, then it's likely there are negative thoughts causing you to waver and beliefs that are holding you back. Rest assured that this is not just you. Every single person on earth has work to do when we decide to change our lives. *The Wiz* shows us the way.

Like Dorothy and her friends, you gotta remember who you are.

You have to learn how to live in alignment with your purpose.

And you have to be courageous in the face of fear.

Questioning what you say, what you think, *what you believe* is part of the process to becoming who you're meant to be. Mind you, that journey doesn't happen within a tidy two hours and 14 minutes like in *The Wiz*. Your shift and growth is going to be gradual, like it was for me and my clients—one Dorothy moment at a time.

But first we have to learn how to dream bigger. You might be dreaming of a trip to Miami, but only because you haven't seen the Maldives yet. (And I say that in my 30s after getting my first passport at 28.) Even though I don't know you, trust me when I say there is a 99 percent chance you are dreaming too small. But in case I haven't convinced you yet, here are some examples of what that looks like.

I just want to be debt-free.

I'd be happy with six figures.

I want to make enough money to take more vacations.

I'd really like to make enough money to leave my job.

If you can't see it yet, all of this is survival. This is oppression showing up and demanding you dream small. To "just" do anything is a four-figure or five-figure mindset. If you've been thinking this way, it's not your fault. You haven't been exposed to different thinking yet. But in this book you will, so these are the kind of statements I want you to interrogate in the future. Remember: Your words reveal your level of thinking, and your thinking shows you what you believe. We must change ourselves at that deep level of belief.

So, let's expose you to some different and possibly new thinking . . .

THE YELLOW BRICK ROAD TO WEALTH

In 2023, I hosted my friend Amelia Thomas at my live event, 7-Figure Educator LIVE. Amelia is a wealth manager with over 20 years' experience in the finance industry, helping first-generation millionaires build nine-figures of wealth (yes, you read that right). In a fireside chat, Amelia mentioned that only 10 percent of the tax code in the United States can be leveraged by W-2 employees. Consequently, there's not a lot that a W-2 employee can do to change how much money they owe in taxes.

Contrast that to the other 90 percent of the tax code, which is dedicated to small business owners, entrepreneurs, and investors. Despite what you might think, the government isn't trying to get us to pay more taxes. It's actually the opposite. The IRS has written the tax code to incentivize people to be small business owners, become entrepreneurs, and invest, because those activities stimulate, support, and grow our economy. That's why research overwhelmingly shows that most business owners pay very little in personal taxes compared to W-2 employees. How much you have to pay in taxes depends on your individual tax situation, but knowing how to take home as much in salary and profit as you can is part of the hidden curriculum within entrepreneurship (that we'll get to later in the book).

Here's a meta moment for you, circling back to an earlier example within this chapter. When I was at the London Business School, none of the successful entrepreneurs I was talking to were worried about retirement. Why? Because they all knew they would have more than enough. That's because there are tax-advantaged retirement accounts for business owners and the self-employed that aren't available to W-2 employees. For example, when I am writing this in 2025, business owners can contribute up to $70,000 in a Simplified Employee Pension (SEP) IRA or Solo 401(k) annually. (This amount changes every year, but it's always to our benefit as business owners.) Back to that educator in New York wanting to secure her own retirement: That means as an entrepreneur, that same educator could invest seven times more in her retirement accounts than she would be able to working for a school district. Plus, both of those contributions (employer and employee) are tax deductible.

I don't know about you, but investing $70,000 annually sounds better for my own retirement than $10,500. This is a very basic example, but what I want you to recognize is that the best and fastest way to build intergenerational, long-term wealth is through owning businesses and later, by investing. And that the government *rewards* us for doing so at every stage of our own growth. You might not have known that until today, and that's okay. We don't know what we don't know. But when we know, we can shift our mindset to dream bigger. As a community, educators, and especially educators of color, get to dream bigger—including by building larger, more lucrative, and more valuable businesses.

A growth moment that all entrepreneurs get to have is glowing up from being an employee to becoming CEO to eventually being a founder. Right before writing this book, I attended a retreat hosted by a mentor of mine who has achieved eight figures and beyond in her business. What I noticed at that retreat was that my mentor knew very little about logistics, planning, or operations. All she knew was that she had this retreat on her calendar for the day, so she showed up with the expectation that her team had all the details handled. She showed up as the founder of her company. Not as the CEO, and certainly not as an employee. In that moment, she represented dreaming bigger—even for me. As the founder, my mentor's schedule was more spacious than mine. (Because at the time, I was operating as the CEO of my company.) While she knew what was happening within her company at a high strategic level, she trusted her team to handle the details. Which in turn allowed her to be creative and show up the way only she could.

Often when educators start businesses, we think and operate like employees. I did, because that's what I knew at the time. Maybe you do too because you don't know anything else. But employees prioritize safety. An employee thinks about that paycheck every two weeks and making sure they do enough to get that money. Not more, not less. Because employees want to feel secure, they avoid risk and are usually pretty okay with complacency. Contrast that to a chief executive officer. CEOs know how to get things done and are focused on prioritizing efficiency. A

CEO creates plans and manages the execution of those plans, including the people who work for and with them. Maybe that CEO is developing frameworks to grow the business, but their thinking is still limited.

A founder considers alignment and prioritizes bigger strategic thinking. Founders love to innovate, and because of that, they don't just lean into risk; they dance with it. Eventually you will be a founder, but you gotta move through the other levels first. These roles—employee, CEO, founder—are also mindsets to adopt and grow out of as your business grows.

This is similar to an idea coined by investor, entrepreneur, and best-selling author Robert Kiyosaki in his book *The Cashflow Quadrant*. In Robert's framework, each of the four quadrants (or roles or mindsets) represents a way that someone could be making money.

Where most people start is as an employee. As an employee, you have a job where your time generates money. When you start your consulting business, you move quadrants because you become self-employed. Kiyosaki describes this as owning a job. That might seem odd, but most solopreneurs don't own a business, per se. Most self-employed people are still trading time for money. If they take a vacation, their business shuts down. They're working a job. The only difference is that you own the job instead of someone else owning it. Ninety-six percent of Black-owned businesses are sole proprietorships, meaning that most are in this quadrant.

The next move, which I'm going to teach you how to do in this book, is to become a business owner. The biggest difference between being self-employed and being a business owner? Ownership.

Business ownership is when you start creating replicable systems and begin building a team. This is when your business becomes an asset in itself. From there you can become an investor, where you own both investments and assets—including your business—that generate money. At that point, you're more showing up like Daymond John on *Shark Tank* or the way my mentor was. You have ideas and insight, but participate at high level rather than managing the day-to-day work.

To wrap your minds around these frameworks, return to the question we started with.

In what quadrant and what mindset are you dreaming?

As an employee? Self-employed? CEO?

If so, you are *still* dreaming too small.

While this book isn't about becoming a founder or investor—yet—my goal is to help you become a true business owner. To do that, you have to create ownership within your business. There are three ways to do that.

Option 1: Ownership through intellectual property

Nobody else can use the term *7-Figure Educator*, because I own it.

Nobody can use the term *Wealthy Black Educator*, because I own it.

Nobody can even operate as "Erica Jordan-Thomas," because I own it (beware bot accounts). And yes, you can own your own name. Which means no one else can use it for commercial purposes.

If you want to use any of those phrases, you have to pay me. Because I own the trademarks. It's my intellectual property. Everything you create that's your own idea, everything that springs from your brain can be owned as intellectual property. Books and e-books, frameworks, patents, inventions, trade secrets, brand names, even the names of your offers, services, and company . . . all of it falls under the umbrella of intellectual property.

Claiming and legally owning what is rightfully yours is an act of social justice. Even though there have been intellectual property protections in the United States since 1790, Black Americans and other folks of color have routinely and often systemically had their creative work copied, stolen, or mismanaged. Consider this example: In 1975, a talent agent named Wally Amos Jr. decided to quit show business and start a cookie shop in Los Angeles using his aunt Della's recipe and a $25,000 loan from friends.

Thanks to Amos's amazing recipe and creative marketing, the Famous Amos Cookie Company generated $300,000 in sales within the first year. By 1982 the company was generating over $12 million in revenue. However, according to the *New York Times*, Amos struggled to keep up profits as the company expanded. He sold off equity stakes throughout the 1980s to keep the company afloat, and in 1988 sold what he had left to a private equity group for approximately $3 million. What Amos didn't realize at the time was that the rights to his name, likeness, and image were included in the deal. This prevented him from selling cookies in the future or even promoting himself as "Famous Amos."

He later told CNBC, "I was stupid, plain and simple. I sold the company and didn't realize I had sold my future along with it." Though Amos was later allowed to create a muffin brand called Uncle Wally, he never recaptured his initial success.

History is full of examples of famous brands based on the likenesses of real people who were never fairly compensated, like Aunt Jemima and Uncle Ben. I don't play with intellectual property, because it's incredibly valuable. Whenever I have an idea for what to name a new offer or event, I'll e-mail my attorney and file a trademark application with a quickness. But you don't even have to go that far when you're just starting out.

An easy way to protect and start owning your intellectual property is to buy domain names for the ideas you have and register the handles on social media. When you name an offer, grab all the relevant domain names (.com, .net, maybe even .org). When you dream up a course, buy those site names too. Take care of the simple stuff now, and when those ideas do come to life, you can file a trademark and be able to show that the idea belongs to you and your business.

Trademark, patent, or copyright?

According to the United States Patent and Trademark Office:

A *trademark* is a word, phrase, design (or combination of all three) that identifies and distinguishes your goods or services. Trademarks prevent other people from passing off your IP as their own.

A *patent* is a technical invention, mechanical process, or machine design that is new, or unique. Patents are meant to protect inventors and are used to protect physical products.

A *copyright* is a created work—like books, music, movies, software code, and visual art—that is original and exists in a tangible medium like paper, canvas, film, or even digitally. Copyright is meant to protect creators and artists from other people stealing or exploiting their work for monetary gain without permission.

Option 2: Ownership through mergers, acquisitions, and creating new entities

A second way to build ownership in your business is through mergers (combining your business with another into a single entity), acquisitions (when you buy another company), and by creating entirely new businesses. While combining, buying, and creating new businesses might seem like an advanced tactic, this type of ownership might be closer than you think. Here's a great example. Part of my business is putting on big, in-person events. As such, one of the biggest expenses in my business is renting event spaces. Earlier in this chapter, I mentioned that I'm about to buy a commercial property—which is actually an *acquisition* for my company. Not only will I save money on expenses for every event we host, but that commercial property and event space could also be a revenue generator when I rent it out to fellow entrepreneurs.

Similarly, I also mentioned before that I own five properties and consequently created a real estate company as a *separate business entity*. I bought my house in Atlanta after I realized it was less expensive to pay a mortgage than to stay in short-term rentals and hotels. Both of my companies benefited from this acquisition. My education consulting business saved money on travel expenses while my real estate business earned revenue renting it out to other folks.

Similarly, a less intense way to create more ownership in your business is to bring services in-house that may be currently contracted with an external vendor. When I launched the *7-Figure Educator* podcast, I partnered with a podcast production company. After three seasons, I realized that we had built an in-house system for content creation, and we had an amazing relationship with a videographer who could edit the podcast. Because of that, we really only needed our podcast producer to distribute the recordings, which we could also do internally. Looking at my expenses for the year, I realized that it would be less expensive to bring production in-house by hiring my own videographer and becoming my own producer. So, that's what I did. As a result, we are in the early stages of building the foundations of a media company that could one day sell our services to someone else.

Keep in mind that creating and managing multiple business entities is an advanced move. Most of the time, it involves a lot of strategy, planning, and financial capital. I'm including it here both as an example and as inspiration for you to envision the future of your business. What other businesses could be complementary to yours? What could you bring in-house? And what type of acquisition, merger, or creation strategy could work for you personally?

Option 3: Ownership through physical assets

This form of ownership, in a lot of ways, is the most obvious. Every physical item you use in your business that has resale value can be considered an asset. While most of us begin by owning equipment that helps us in our business, we can expand beyond that. As your business (and profit) grows, managing how much you owe in taxes will become really important. That's because most small businesses are structured as pass-through companies, meaning that all the profit you earn from your business "passes through" to your personal tax return. That's not such a big deal when you're making five figures, but when you have seven figures in annual revenue with 30 precent profit . . . that's $300,000 (or more) of taxable income.

There are multiple ways to mitigate your tax liability as a business owner, but my personal favorite that adds ownership is buying real estate. As of 2025, there is a tax loophole for short-term rental properties (like Airbnbs or Vrbos) that allows owners to write off the full depreciation for the property in the first year. This is a big deal, because instead of using a portion of the value as a business expense every year for 30 years, I can apply the full value of the property as an expense in year one. That will reduce the taxes I owe that calendar year and often helps me avoid a big tax bill.

I want to be real with you and admit that I personally wouldn't have bought all the properties I have just to be a real estate investor. My short-term rental business makes far less in revenue and profit than my education consulting business. But the amount that business provides me personally in tax savings is well worth it. Understanding the fact that the United States tax code is written to benefit small business owners and investors is part of the hidden curriculum both in business ownership and intergenerational wealth.

Regardless of where you are in your business journey, you can become an owner.

Right now. Today.

An accessible way to start is by creating intellectual property. That's literally free. In fact, I bet you probably already *have* intellectual property, even if it's not yet formally protected through the U.S. Patent and Trademark Office. Start dreaming big by considering what mergers and acquisitions, what physical assets would be complementary and beneficial to your business. Start thinking about ownership now, because that's what will move you from being an employee or self-employed (where you must exchange time for money) to becoming a business owner, a CEO, and then later, an investor and founder (owning the systems that generate money). Ownership is a path to long-term, sustainable wealth and the freedom that comes with having that wealth, which is why we create businesses in the first place.

DREAMING BIGGER

Research has demonstrated that when we see someone like us succeeding, we begin to believe it's possible for ourselves. In this chapter (and continuing through the whole book), I'm showing you what's possible. Now that you know *how* to dream bigger, you can start to envision what you want and plan how you'll get there. We're going to do that right now with two important steps to making your dreams a reality. As I mentioned at the beginning of this chapter, you'll start by identifying two essential guideposts:

First, calculate your **Freedom Number**. That's the amount of money you need to pay your bills and keep a roof over your head. Your Freedom Number may also enable you to leave your current job, if that's what you want. (More on that choice in a minute.)

Second, figure out your **Abundance Number**, or what your dream lifestyle actually costs (which might not be as much as you expect).

Putting real math behind these goals is going to be a Dorothy moment for you, so grab a pen and plan a little celebration for yourself, because we're about to dream BIG.

CALCULATING YOUR FREEDOM NUMBER

Your Freedom Number is the dollar amount your business must make annually in order to replace your salary. But this number represents more than just being able to leave your job. When you hit or exceed your own Freedom Number, you will have put your own financial safety, security, and success in your own hands. Hitting your Freedom Number is the moment your job *needs* you more than you need them. And that feels damn good whether you leave your job or not.

The easy way to calculate your Freedom Number is to double the salary you're trying to earn.

So, if you would want to pay yourself $50,000 a year, your business would need to earn $100,000 in revenue ($50K x 2) annually to meet your Freedom Number, or about $8,335 monthly. This calculation is based on the Profit First method created by best-selling author Mike Michalowicz. According to Michalowicz, businesses earning up to $250,000 in revenue should allocate 50 percent of money earned to owners' comp (i.e., the amount of money you pay yourself from your business).

Note that I say *desired* salary. You could use your current salary to calculate your Freedom Number, but that's not dreaming big. Nor is it setting your business up to grow and be successful. If you're early in your business's journey, you might have been able to pocket every dollar that has come in because you aren't earning all that much money, your expenses are low, and there aren't many surprises at tax time. But that's not going to be the case when you start using this book and earning more. Dream bigger and set yourself up for success.

Solid financial structures are crucial for your growth, and are much easier to create when you're starting out than to fix later. Making sure you start managing the money coming into your business with your Freedom Number in mind is going to help you reach that goal faster. And you want that to happen quickly. Because the moment you hit that number, when your business is able to pay you the same amount of money that you're taking home from an employer . . . there's gonna be a shift. The energy and emotion when that happens is hard to put words to, but the whole vibe changes. You won't need a job to feel safe. Mind you, you might still choose to show up. But you won't *have* to, and that's the difference.

Is there really a conflict of interest?

I don't have an opinion on whether or not you should stay at your job. But I do want you to experience your full financial potential, which will not be at your job.

If you love what you do and don't want to leave your current 9-to-5 to build your business—that's okay. It's possible to do both. In fact, I have several clients who earn over $100,000 in their businesses *while* working full-time jobs. One of my most successful clients runs a multi-six-figure business providing training for leaders of special education departments in large school districts—*while* holding a 9-to-5 administrative role for a charter school company. It is doable.

However, if you're considering staying at your job while also running a business, there are a few steps you need to take. First, take the time to get really clear on what your employee contract says. Some organizations do have clauses that restrict you from working elsewhere or in similar fields, but many do not.

It's worth finding out what is actually in the contract you signed, because often, even the most diligent educators forget what's on that paper. I don't know how many times a client of mine has assumed there was a conflict or a restriction when there wasn't. If the contract is fuzzy around what you can and can't do, talk to your HR department. Do your due diligence.

If you do have a restriction in your employment contract or there's an obvious conflict of interest, revisit your goals. If your goal is to stay at your job, then you may have to pivot what you aim to provide in your business. That said, if your goal is to eventually *leave* your job, that pivot might only be temporary.

CALCULATING YOUR ABUNDANCE NUMBER

An important facet to dreaming big is thinking with abundance. That can feel foreign to educators because we've constantly been asked and expected to accept less than we deserve, financially and otherwise.

For the next exercise, I encourage you to consider what *abundance* really means and looks like to you. For example, what is your dream home? A ranch set on multiple acres in your home state? A condo steps from the beach in Miami? Maybe it's multiple homes where you can escape the weather or the city or just get away.

Similarly, what kind of lifestyle do you desire? How many vacations do you want to take, and where? Do you want a private chef? A stylist? A personal trainer? In-home childcare? Educational opportunities for yourself or your kids? Do you want to outsource your laundry? Go to the spa once a month, once a week, once a quarter? Does someone do your grocery shopping for you? Do you always want to sit in the good seats at concerts, sporting events, the theater? What kind of car do you dream about driving? Is it a drop-top? A Tesla? The newest Benz?

Beyond the lifestyle questions, what do you want to do with all the money and wealth you're creating? Do you want to donate regularly to charities, max out your contributions for retirement, own multiple properties? Do you want a financial planner, trusts for your family, a foundation?

These are just a few areas to consider. Your dreams might include more, or your goals might be totally different. Take your time, think expansively, and try to capture as much detail as you can. You can revise your personal idea of abundance anytime, so don't get caught up trying to make it perfect. Once you've got your dream life roughly sketched out, start researching costs. If you want to drive a Benz, calculate the monthly payment. If you want a monthly chef, google a local catering company and get a quote. If you want to buy multiple properties, search real estate sites to figure out an estimated monthly cost. (AI tools are great for this kind of rough math.)

Once you have all the costs, add them up. Then complete these sentences:

THE ANNUAL COST OF MY ABUNDANT LIFESTYLE IS _______________________,
(THIS IS YOUR ABUNDANCE NUMBER.)

Your Abundance Number is now the money you ultimately want to generate and take home from your business. (Note that this likely won't be your salary or represent 50 percent of annual revenue, for reasons I'll get into later.) If you are surprised by the figure, that's normal. Every time I teach this exercise at 7-Figure Educator LIVE, people are shocked to find their dream life is closer and easier to realize than they assumed.

Sometimes—let's be real, a lot of the time—we assume that we have to be millionaires to experience luxury. But the moment I realized meal delivery costs the same as groceries, or that wash-and-fold with door-to-door service was literally the price of detergent, I switched up quick.

When I first calculated my own Abundance Number, my dream life cost $300,000 per year. Which, as it turns out, was completely doable. In fact, my initial abundance goals are pretty much how I live my life today. I own a few properties that I travel between, I donate to charity, I spend money on the vacations I want. And, most importantly, I feel like I have enough in the bank to do what I want to do.

The power in calculating your Abundance Number is to see that you are closer than you might think to what you've been dreaming of. Often $250,000 or $300,000 is more than enough to get you everything you want and more. That's totally possible for you, especially now that you have this book.

CHAPTER 2 REFLECTION QUESTIONS

1. How have you been dreaming small?

2. Which of the identities (Scarecrow, Tinman, cowardly Lion) do you most resonate with?

3. What do you and/or your business own, if anything?

4. What *could* your business own in the future in terms of intellectual property, mergers and acquisitions, or physical assets?

5. What is the gap between your current revenue/ salary and your Freedom Number?

6. What do you need to believe about yourself in order to reach your Freedom Number? How about your Abundance Number?

ACTION STEPS

- Calculate your Freedom Number.
- Calculate your Abundance Number.

7-FIGURE EDUCATOR RESOURCES

Visit **www.7febook.com/resources** to:

- Grab a copy of *Profit First* by Mike Michalowicz
- Grab a copy of *The Cashflow Quadrant* by Robert Kiyosaki
- Watch Episode 15: "How to Build Your Money Team & Leverage Your Assets Like The 1% with Amelia Thomas" of the *7-Figure Educator* podcast to continue to be exposed to next-level money beliefs
- Watch Episode 18: "Resilience in Rhinestones: How to Build a Million Dollar Business with Dr. Traci Lynn" of the *7-Figure Educator* podcast to continue to stretch your money mindsets

99 Problems...
but You Gotta Pick One

Objective: Identify the problem that your business will solve

Now that you've got your Freedom Number and your Abundance Number, we can move on to building the business that makes those numbers show up in your bank account. The first step is with choosing and defining the one problem your business will solve. Yes, I said *one*.

That might sound revolutionary.

That might challenge what you think you know about entrepreneurship.

That might run counter to what you've seen on social media about building wealth.

But it's the key to your business's growth and your financial freedom.

Solving *one* problem is going to be different from anything you've done before as an educator. I don't know of any profession, any area of expertise, or any job that requires as many *skills* as teaching.

As educators—at any level—we need to:

- master effective pedagogy through strong use of curriculum design and differentiated instruction;

- be able to communicate effectively with students, parents, teachers, administrators, and the broader community;

- manage our classroom environment through daily routines, discipline, and activities;

- develop high-quality assessments aligned to content standards;

- build trusting relationships so that we can motivate students and ensure their performance, individually and collectively, meets or exceeds expectations; and

- so much more . . .

Every teacher I know can do all of that, at the same time, *while* being surrounded by 30+ kids who each have their own unique interests and attitudes about learning. One of my favorite frameworks to illustrate all the components of effective teaching was created by Research for Better Teaching, an OG in the world of education consulting.

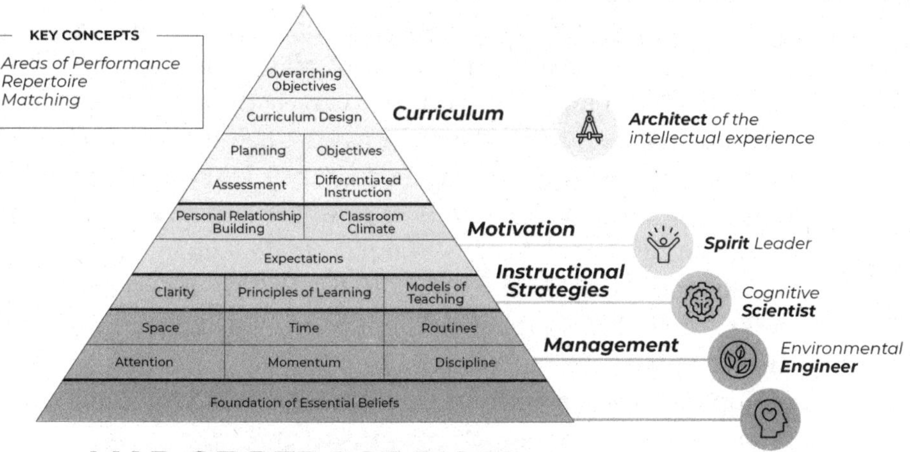

MAP OF PEDAGOGICAL KNOWLEDGE

It's their pyramid of pedagogical knowledge, and I'm sharing the visual only as a reminder of what you are already proficient at.

You can literally do it all.

In fact, you *have*.

As an educator, you don't have the privilege of compartmentalizing. You've been solving multiple problems and floating in between tasks and stakeholders and solutions for as long as you've been teaching, and you're damn good at it.

But when it comes to creating a business, doing it all is no longer an asset.

As entrepreneurs, we can't wear all the problem-solving hats we did as educators.

Jay-Z might have had 99 problems, but we can't, my friend. We shouldn't be solving everything for anybody. Instead, we need to focus on solving one problem at a time in our business to create the success we want.

I want to get out ahead of your fear and acknowledge that narrowing your focus to solving only one problem at a time can feel incredibly scary when you are used to being the person who fixes everything for everybody. Picking just one problem feels hard when you haven't had the privilege of choice before. After all, most educators I know don't get to say, "I want to do instructional planning, but I'll pass on family engagement." Instead, you have to do it all and do it well in order to be effective. Don't even get me started on that pesky "other duties as assigned" line in the job offer, or how most of us have the experience of being expected to thrive in multiple roles—often in multiple classrooms or even multiple schools—at once. (Shoutout to my floaters.)

Honestly, trying to do all the things is a form of overworking. Take the analogy of teaching multiple preps. As a high school math teacher, I taught two to three different preps each semester. Which meant every day, I had two to three lesson plans, two to three exit tickets, two to three quizzes, two to three guided notes, etc. I dreamed of being responsible for just one prep. Picking one problem to solve in your business is like teaching just one prep. Trying to solve multiple problems is like teaching multiple preps, and I don't know anyone who would *choose* that life.

Feeling resistance and fear around focusing on a single area within your business makes sense. However, what I know as a business coach and as an entrepreneur myself is that getting specific on the problem you want to solve will not only help you go further faster but will make the daily work in your business easier.

Let me break it down for you. Being focused on one specific problem will help you identify your ideal client with ease, determine what to say yes to and what to politely decline, and establish a business model that works for your strengths and creates the tangible results your business promises. The one problem you choose to solve will become your North Star and be the foundation of everything you do.

This chapter is all about helping you to choose the one problem your business will solve.

One. Not two, not three. Not 10, not 50, and certainly not 99. Because each of those little squares on the pyramid from RBT could be a million-dollar business all by itself. When I teach this concept, I often bring up two hugely successful companies: Amazon and Partake Foods.

When Jeff Bezos started Amazon in 1994, he wasn't trying to sell books, air fryers, groceries, leggings, or whatever else is in your weekly Prime delivery. Instead, he was trying to figure out a way to get customers to buy products online. He *started* with books because he knew there was a customer problem to solve. Then and now, brick-and-mortar bookstores offered a limited selection in store because it is impossible to stock every book a reader could potentially want. By providing access to an infinitely broader selection online, Amazon was able to offer customers what physical retail could not. Within 30 days, Amazon was generating $20,000 in weekly revenue.

Similarly, when executive Denise Woodward found out that her one-year-old daughter had severe food allergies (to tree nuts, eggs, corn, and bananas) she felt anxious and scared. Seeing that there were limited packaged-food options that were safe for her daughter, Woodward saw an opportunity to create a brand that would be safe for people with allergies while also appealing to a broad audience of consumers. She launched Partake Foods in 2017 with cookies that were gluten-free, non-GMO, vegan, and did not contain the top nine allergens (wheat, tree nuts, peanuts, milk, eggs, soy, fish, sesame, and shellfish). As of 2023, products from Partake Foods are carried in more than 12,000 stores nationwide, including Kroger, Target, Walmart, and Whole Foods Market—solving a serious problem for the 33 million Americans who have a food allergy. (Notice how sis didn't buy into that "Well, the cookie market is already saturated" BS!)

I share these examples to model three things:

First, solving a seemingly simple problem can be incredibly lucrative. Second, even the simplest problems can have a huge impact on people. And last, the problem that you set out to solve isn't always the only problem you can end up solving. Jeff Bezos may have created an online bookstore, *and* his business answered the question of whether people would shop online. Denise Woodward may have created tasty products for people who didn't have enough snack options, *and* by doing so, created safe alternatives for Black children who are more likely to both have allergies and experience reactions that require emergency care.

The focus is tight, but the impact can be far-reaching. I'm going to help you use all your resources to think creatively and expansively about what problem your business is going to solve. We're not trying to find the absolute perfect solution that's going to build your multimillion-dollar empire tomorrow, but the goal is to identify your one problem and go from there. Follow these four prompts:

1. Identify your areas of expertise.

2. Find what makes you float.

3. Choose and define the problem your business will solve.

4. Pull your receipts.

One income stream at a time . . . .

When I mentioned Jeff Bezos, I didn't mention Alexa or Blue Origin. While I talked about Denise Woodward, I didn't mention that she expanded into waffle mixes and graham crackers as additional product lines to her cookies. Or that she created Black Futures in Food & Beverage, a fellowship program that mentors HBCU students, helping them to secure internships and jobs in the food and beverage industry. That's because founders—true founders—don't start with multiple ideas and side projects. Instead, what I want you to recognize is that those founders figured out how to solve *one* problem first.

This messaging might go against what you've heard about building wealth. You might be thinking, ***Dr. EJT, I heard that I need seven streams of income to be a millionaire.*** Welcome to lesson #2 of the hidden curriculum of entrepreneurship that I mentioned earlier.

"Seven streams of income" is getting a lot of play online because it is a legitimate strategy to build wealth. That said, it is also one of those concepts that gets distorted. Remember the game of telephone as a kid? How the message would get garbled after passing from person to person to person? That's what is happening here.

The original source of the seven-streams-of-income concept is the Bible. In case you didn't catch it already, I'm a God girl. And while I'm never going to try to convert you, I will drop Bible verses where appropriate.

Ecclesiastes 11:2 says, "Divide your portion to seven, or even to eight, for you do not know what misfortune may occur on the earth" (New American Standard Bible).

Basically, it's smart to be diversified financially. This advice from biblical times is still valid.

But over time, this wisdom got twisted. Some people now think they have to *start* with seven income streams to become millionaires. But splitting your focus and efforts before you've even gotten one stream of income off the ground is the exact opposite of what to do.

Instead, focus on one thing at a time, with this book as your step-by-step guide. Once you've identified your one problem, started the business that will solve that problem, and your first income stream is stable, use that success as a blueprint to create another income stream. Simply rinse and repeat until you have seven, eight, or as many income streams as you want and need.

STEP 1: IDENTIFY YOUR AREAS OF EXPERTISE

It's often hard to parse what we truly love about education. Is it the kids? Lesson planning? Geeking out about pedagogy? Supporting inclusion practices? Being in community with other teachers and helping them to thrive?

In working with hundreds of clients, I've figured out a way for you to find your own answers. There are four expert zones worthy of exploring:

1. Content/Subject areas

2. Grade levels

3. Professional skills

4. Student/Staff subgroups

Four questions to ask yourself:

Expertise Question #1: What are the content areas and subjects I am experienced in? For example: literacy, chemistry, algebra 2, special education, physical education, social-emotional learning (SEL)

Expertise Question #2: How about grade levels of expertise? Get specific here: K–2, 9th–12th grade, early childhood, higher education

Expertise Question #3: What skills do I have? For example: classroom management, ACT prep, family engagement, culturally relevant pedagogy

Expertise Question #4: What subgroups of students/staff have an extra-special place in my heart? Not saying we have favorites (or maybe we do!) but we usually have an extra superpower with a particular subgroup. Get specific here too: English as a second language (ESL), Black boys, students who qualify for free and reduced lunch, gifts-and-talents students, first-year teachers, first-year principals, etc.

SUBJECTS/ CONTENT AREAS EXPERTISE	SKILLS	REVENUE GENERATING?
Algebra 1 and Geometry	Creating engaging math lessons and activities that get students involved and learning	Middle and high school students (Grades 6-12) Students assigned to alternative learning settings

Be generative. You should have a list under each question. The goal in choosing one problem your business will solve is to start making money. There's no need to know today exactly what you're going to do forever or what's going to make you millions. Instead, treat this first problem you identify as an experiment. Because you are likely to refine this idea or even pivot entirely once you know more than you know today. Instead of trying to be perfect, I encourage you to pick your problem and go get a client or contract within the next 30 days. Remember, the real objective of this chapter (and ultimately this book) is to help you prove to yourself that you can make money. The longer you hem and haw over this decision, the longer you're holding off on proving to yourself that you can make money . . . which is the key ingredient to create the momentum to keep going.

This is one of the many points in the book where I'm going to ask you to slay your own perfectionism, because the problem you pick doesn't have to be perfect. No one's grading you on it except for yourself. Give yourself permission to treat this as an experiment in science class. You're simply choosing a hypothesis to try, and if you get data that tells you to pivot, you'll choose another and repeat until you find your sweet spot.

Now that I'm done telling you it's okay to be imperfect, let me show you how answering these questions leads you to the problem your business will solve in real life. After serving in the military, my client Jayson got a degree in education. His first assignment was at an alternative school. But this wasn't a charter or magnet school for traditional students. Instead, Jayson worked with students who were at risk of expulsion, on long-term suspension from their original high schools, or both. He couldn't teach math the old, archaic way, because lecturing could create safety issues.

Like so many educators, Jayson had to get creative. He started designing board games and other math manipulatives to get students engaged in learning. Within weeks, his students were showing improvement, and by the end of his first semester, Jayson knew that his ideas had paid off.

Fast-forward to today, where Jayson has created a business teaching districts how to incorporate his fun, engaging math manipulatives into classrooms.

Here are some examples of Jayson's answers to those earlier Expertise Questions:

Expertise Question #1: What are the content areas and subjects I am experienced in?

Algebra I and geometry

Expertise Question #2: How about grade levels?

I have experience working with middle and high school students (Grades 6–12).

Expertise Question #3: What skills do I have?

I can create engaging math lessons and activities that get students involved and learning.

Expertise Question #4: What groups of students am I the best at helping?

Students assigned to alternative learning settings

You should have a list of answers like these for each Expertise Question. This list can and should be long. Often my clients end up with 50 to 60 answers between the four questions. Once you have your answers, you can move to the next step.

STEP 2: FIND WHAT MAKES YOU FLOAT

Now it's time to refine even more. I'm going to share with you a framework that I have found to be very helpful in getting clarity on the one problem that you're solving in your business. It's from an amazing book called *The Big Leap* by Gay Hendricks. In that book, he says people tend to have four zones of competence when it comes to tasks (particularly at work):

1. The Zone of Incompetence: tasks you simply aren't good at

2. The Zone of Competence: tasks you are good at, but don't enjoy

3. The Zone of Excellence: tasks you're good at, enjoy doing, and are used to doing well professionally . . . but they feel like work when you do them

4. The Zone of Genius: tasks you enjoy so much that you lose track of time

For our purposes, we're going to focus on the last two zones.

In *The Big Leap*, Hendricks is clear that the Zone of Excellence is a perfectly good place to be. After all, you've put time and practice into building those skills. You are legitimately so good within your Zone of Excellence that you likely receive compliments and accolades on that work. Many of the educators I work with say that their 9-to-5 job is within this zone. It's very comfortable to stay within the Zone of Excellence, because you're good at that work and it benefits the people around you. Oftentimes, work that falls within this zone doesn't really feel like hard work because it comes so easy to you.

But your Zone of Excellence is not what you are absolutely the best at. Because that work falls in your Zone of Genius. Your genius is where your innate abilities, your unique personality, and your experience and skills combine to reach that magical level of flow. Nobody else can do your Zone of Genius the way you do. That's why the book is called *The Big Leap*—because it's all about moving from spending most of your time comfortable but not challenged in your Zone of Excellence to creating a joyful business and satisfying life around your Zone of Genius.

You might be thinking, *Awesome, I'm just going to work in my Zone of Genius, then.*

While that is the goal (and the whole reason I'm mentioning this framework in the first place), it can be tricky to differentiate between your Zone of Excellence and your Zone of Genius. Remember, the tasks that fall into both categories are all things you do really well. The difference between the two zones is how you *feel* while doing those tasks. You may feel confident and capable while working in your Zone of Excellence, but when you're in your Zone of Genius . . . you feel like you're floating. A big clue that you're in your Zone of Excellence is that whatever you're doing still feels like work. You might be good at it, but that 'ish takes effort.

Sometimes, it can be helpful to visualize what's in your Zone of Excellence and what is your Zone of Genius. First, revisit your answers to the Expertise Questions I previously shared. Remember, each answer is an area of your expertise. Next, consider the *intersections* of your areas of expertise to identify the problem your business can solve. In this exercise, I use a Venn diagram, but you can use whatever is most helpful to you. The intention of this exercise is to see where your expert zones intersect. In the illustration on the next page, I've used stars to show where the overlap is.

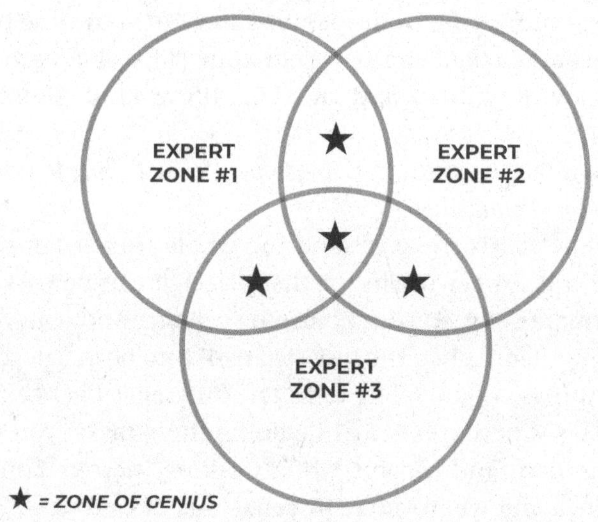

Going back to Jayson, his expert zones were working with students in alternative learning settings, high school–level math, and creating math manipulatives. You and I both know that lots of people are great at teaching in alternative settings. Similarly, plenty of folks want to support high school students with math, and many education consultants work in the classroom.

These areas of expertise are powerful on their own, but when you intersect them, you become a unicorn like Jayson.

The final step in identifying your Zone of Genius is to understand which specific intersection makes you float. I find the easiest way to do this is to map out all the intersections and then to *feel* your way through each of them. Alternatively, you can also choose one area of expertise or skill from each of your expert zones.

Working with Jayson, we identified that out of all the teaching he did, *creating math manipulatives* was what felt the easiest and most rewarding. Next, he told me that while working in alternative educational settings was fulfilling and impactful, he wished more secondary teachers would make learning math fun. And last, sharing his manipulatives in the classroom lit him up in a way that teaching in traditional ways simply didn't.

Jayson's Zone of Genius was: Lesson planning + math manipulatives + 6–12 grades

Let's go through another example: me. When I started my business, I had a doctorate in education leadership as well as experience working as an educator, a principal, an education consultant, and as an entrepreneur. I also have a level of expertise around equity and belonging—academically as a student, as a practitioner that led equity work, and as someone who studied for my dissertation how equity and belonging exist (or don't) within systems.

All those areas of expertise are in my Zones of Excellence—that's why people wanted to hire me to help them with their businesses. But even though staying within those zones would be lucrative, I wasn't interested. I knew that being a traditional business coach didn't light me up. Though I love education, I didn't want to be limited to working with schools and districts. And while facilitating equity-and-belonging work was rewarding, I didn't feel like I was floating when I was on those stages.

Looking at my diagram, I was able to see an opportunity that would combine all my expert zones into my own unique Zone of Genius. As it turns out, the intersection of where I was able to be excellent—Education + Consulting + Equity & Belonging—was simply the stepping stone to being able to combine all those skills into a unique problem only I could solve.

(Helping educators like you.)

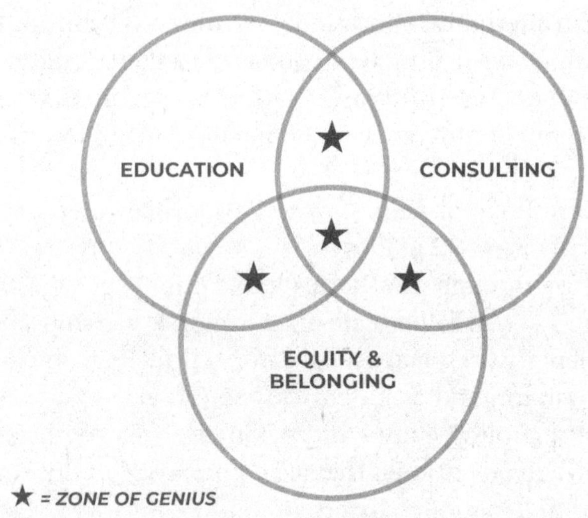

At 7-Figure Educator, our mission is to disrupt the racial wealth gap by shifting power and helping Black educators and educators of color get paid. When I get on stage at 7-Figure Educator LIVE, go on Instagram to drop some gems in a reel, or teach within my mastermind, I do feel like I'm floating. That's because when I do all those things, I'm at *the intersection* of all my expertise rather than compartmentalizing and focusing on only one zone at a time.

Now it's your turn. When you craft your Venn diagram (or however you want to visualize this concept), think about your own intersection points. You'll notice that in my diagram, I actually have four intersection points. I chose the intersection in the middle, but I could have chosen any one of them. I could have combined Consulting with Equity & Belonging, or Equity & Belonging and Education. The objective of this exercise is to identify the intersection where you feel like you float, where there's energy, where time flies by, where your experience flows. Where you can find the motivation to work on your business even after a long day at your 9-to-5, because it makes you energized. Once you have an idea of what your Zone of Genius is, move to the next step.

You're not the first to do this

Gloria Richardson was a fearless civil rights leader who played a pivotal role in the Cambridge movement of the 1960s, fighting for racial justice and economic equality in Maryland. In one of the most iconic photographs of the era, Richardson is captured walking calmly past a National Guardsman pointing a rifle fixed with a bayonet directly at her. When later asked if she was afraid in that moment, she replied: "I was too upset to be afraid."

Her words offer a powerful lesson for entrepreneurs. When you're identifying the problem your business will solve, look for the one that stirs you so deeply that fear takes a back seat. The right problem to build around is often the one that frustrates, angers, or moves you so much that hesitation isn't even an option.

STEP 3: CHOOSE AND DESCRIBE THE PROBLEM YOUR BUSINESS WILL SOLVE

There's a quote from *Harvard Business Review* that I often share in my programs.

"When developing new products, processes, or even businesses, most companies aren't sufficiently rigorous in defining the problems they're attempting to solve and articulating why those issues are important. Without that rigor, organizations miss opportunities, waste resources, and end up pursuing innovation initiatives that aren't aligned with their strategies."

In short: Identifying the problem your business will solve isn't enough.

You also have to be able to define that problem for other people, who might not understand it as well as you do or be aware that it is a problem at all. Get super familiar with your problem—what it looks like, what it feels like, and its consequences. The clearer you can be around the problem that you're solving, the easier the work going forward will be.

So, what's the one problem your business is going to solve?

At this point you have a list of *potential* problems you could solve (Step 1), as well as an understanding of your areas of expertise and where those overlap into your unique Zone of Genius (Step 2). Yay, you! Let's keep going.

Typically for the educators I work with, this whole process requires a lot of deep reflection. Partly because most educators haven't had a lot of opportunities to make our own choices. And partly because humans are multifaceted and multitalented. You could be successful at a lot of different things, and you could solve a lot of different problems.

I want to reassure you: If you feel like there isn't a singular problem jumping out at you right away or if you're not sure exactly what your Zone of Genius is—you'll get there.

What to do when you get stuck

Notice that I say *when*, not *if*.

As an entrepreneur, you're going to get stuck. Maybe you're stuck right now. Maybe your brain goes blank when you try to think about what problems you could solve, or you're not sure what your Zone of Genius is. Lucky for you, I've seen that before. And often. A great way to get yourself unstuck at this stage is to ask trusted colleagues and friends for help.

> You can ask them: "What do I do really well?"
>
> Or, even better: "What do I do that feels like magic to other people?"
>
> Their answers will tell you a lot and will likely give you inspiration on what to do next.

I want to give you permission to do everything I'm asking you to do *imperfectly*.

The biggest roadblock by far I see among my clients is that they become so overwhelmed by perfectionism at every step that accomplishing anything takes them months rather than days. I don't want that for you. So, when you choose a problem to solve and draft a problem statement, think of it as just a starting point. Everything I'm asking you to do in this chapter and throughout this book is a draft. These are working versions. Give yourself a lot of grace, because the most important part is that you keep it moving.

I want you to choose a problem that lights you up and suits your Zone of Genius. Once you've got that, we can start defining the problem—getting that deep clarity I mentioned at the beginning of the chapter. We do that by drafting a problem description, which has three parts: Consequences, Emotional Impact, and Evidence. And yes, I've got a framework for that. Let's move through it step-by-step.

THE 7-FIGURED™ PROBLEM

Paint a picture of the problem

1. What are the consequences of solving / not solving this problem?

2. What are the emotions associated with the problem? How does this problem make your client feel?

3. What evidence supports that this problem exists?

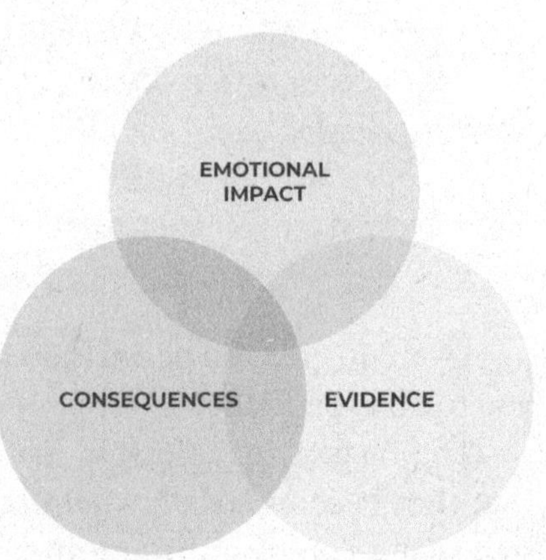

Consequences

To help you paint the picture of the problem, I want you to think about its consequences, and, more importantly, the *emotions* that come along with those consequences. Get real with this and avoid jargon where you can. For example, if the problem your business solves is students not reading at grade level, you could say your business "would address suffering literacy data," or you could say, "Without the work we do, we would miss the opportunity for every student in our school to get lost in a book and learn to love their imagination." Which is more impactful?

Consider: If this problem continues to persist, what are the real-life consequences? And then conversely, if and when the problem is solved, what would that look like? What are those outcomes? Take time to consider both sides. For example, in diversity, equity, and inclusion (DEI) work—if every child were to engage with a culturally responsive curriculum, what would the consequences be? Building on the earlier advice to consider the real and emotional impacts, you could say the consequences might be "students thriving academically and socially as a result of seeing themselves in their curriculum" or "students of color feeling seen, heard, and represented, and more students who are traditionally overlooked believing in their dreams, applying to college, and getting accepted."

Remember, being clear on the consequences gives the people you aim to work with the motivation and urgency to solve the problem (and to hire you to do it).

Emotional Impact

When you think about the problem from the perspective of your target client, what are the emotions associated with the problem? How does this problem make your client feel? When you talk about your business, considering your client's emotions is going to help you make a connection with them. If you're working with first-year teachers, for example, you might acknowledge that they might feel like they are failing every single day when they leave school. Keep in mind, the goal isn't to make anyone feel bad; instead, it's to make a potential client feel seen and think, *They get me, they understand what I'm going through.*

Evidence

This one is simple. What evidence supports that this problem exists? Obviously, you know personally that whatever problem your business is gonna solve exists, but what we're looking for here is *outside* evidence that gives context, that helps show that the problem is happening at scale. That's what provides the incentive and the sense of urgency from your target client to solve the problem.

Let's walk through two examples of what a problem description looks like, and how these three levers of our framework—consequences, emotions, and evidence—show up. In my personal consulting business, I provide coaching and professional development for school leaders. My problem description is as follows:

> Sixty-seven percent of principals agree that typical leadership programs and graduate schools of education are out of touch with the realities of what it takes to run today's school districts.
>
> The average principal is hired into their role underprepared, handed the keys to their building, and expected to lead with little onboarding or support. Today's principals are overwhelmed by the responsibilities of the role and lack access to quality professional development. If this problem persists, principals will continue to leave their schools after three years, and our schools will continue to struggle in meeting the needs of all students.

We can examine how our framework shows up here. While it's not first in this paragraph—and doesn't have to be—the consequences are: *If this problem persists, principals will continue to leave their schools after three years, and our schools will continue to struggle in meeting the needs of all students.* Note that I took the approach of naming the consequences if the problem is not solved. You could do that, *or* you could name what the consequences will be when the problem is solved. If I were to take that tack, I would say, *When this problem is solved, schools will retain their principals beyond the current average of three years and be able to better support students.*

Next, let's look for emotional impact. It's in the second paragraph. *Today's principals are overwhelmed by the responsibilities of the role and lack access to quality professional development.* I'm naming the emotion my target audience is feeling. They're overwhelmed. By describing how my target client is feeling in an accurate way, I'm able to show I understand them and make a stronger connection with that client.

Last, evidence. *Sixty-seven percent of principals agree that typical leadership programs and graduate schools of education are out of touch with the realities of what it takes to run today's school districts.* I chose to start my problem statement with a statistic because it's a cut-and-dry description of what the problem is. To get this, you might need to do research. The evidence you need to support that the problem you want your business to solve *is* urgent and necessary is out there. Maybe it's a study, a white paper, a survey, a government report, or the results of standardized testing. The only requirement is that it's evidence supporting that a problem exists and needs to be solved.

Here's another example from a client:

According to a 2012 survey by the American Federation of Teachers, 1 in 3 teachers felt unprepared to teach on their first day and a 2014 survey by Teach Plus found that 75 percent of teachers reported they were inadequately prepared to meet the needs of their students during their first year. Teachers embark on their journey full of excitement and hope that they'll make a difference in students' lives. Unfortunately, it doesn't take long for them to realize that they are ill equipped for this work. This results in them feeling overwhelmed, ineffective, and defeated. If this problem persists, teachers will continue to leave the profession at alarming rates. Current statistics show that new teachers leave at rates of somewhere between 19 percent and 30 percent within their first five years of teaching. High teacher turnover undermines student achievement. In fact, research shows that high teacher turnover rates negatively impact student achievement for all students in a school; not just those in a new teacher's classroom. Without sustained, school-based professional development guided by expert colleagues responsive to teachers' needs and continual throughout their early years in the classroom, the problem compounds.

Let's walk through how this problem description uses that same framework. The consequences are: *If this problem persists, teachers will continue to leave the profession at alarming rates.* You could flip these consequences to be positive. That would look like this: *When this problem is solved, more new teachers will stay in the profession and improve student outcomes.*

Next, let's look for the emotional connection. This is tricky because this particular problem description is full of feelings—"unprepared," "excitement," "hope"—but the emotional impact here is actually "this results in them feeling overwhelmed, ineffective, and defeated." Remember that the connection you're trying to make in the problem description is the feeling your target client has before they know you exist.

Last, this problem description has lots of evidence.

According to a 2012 survey by the American Federation of Teachers, 1 in 3 teachers felt unprepared to teach on their first day and a 2014 survey by Teach Plus found that 75 percent of teachers reported they were inadequately prepared to meet the needs of their students during their first year. . . . Current statistics show that new teachers leave at rates of somewhere between 19 percent and 30 percent their first five years of teaching. High teacher turnover undermines student achievement. In fact, research shows that high teacher turnover rates negatively impact student achievement for all students in a school; not just those in a new teacher's classroom.

This particular client nailed the urgency with their last sentence: *Without sustained, school-based professional development guided by expert colleagues responsive to teachers' needs and continual throughout their early years in the classroom, the problem compounds.*

When you have a draft of a problem description, it's time to outline a problem statement.

Your problem statement is a one-sentence summary of what your business does. You can think of this as a punchy elevator pitch that you can use when you're meeting someone new at a conference or social function. Don't get caught up in making it perfect. You will refine this as you work in and on your business. Here are examples related to the businesses we just talked about.

For my personal consulting business:

The problem my business is solving is the gap in quality principal professional development.

For my client's business helping new teachers:

The problem my business is solving is the gap in quality professional development for early-career teachers in years one through three.

STEP 4: PULL YOUR RECEIPTS

Now that you have identified your problem statement and description, we need to grab some receipts that show why you are the big (not the lil') one to solve this problem. These receipts will serve as the foundation of your marketing message (more in Chapter 9) that will help you articulate why *you* are the one to solve this problem. You can use my R-E-S framework:

Receipts, aka your results: What results have you gotten in your career that will matter to potential clients and customers? What results prove your ability to create an impact with the work you do?

Experience: Which of your experiences are relevant to the problems you could solve in your business?

Skills: What skills do you bring to the problems that you've identified so far?

My client Tanisha was a former high school counselor who knew that parents and families were often overwhelmed by the college admissions process and frequently left thousands of dollars of scholarship money on the table. She wanted to solve that problem by using her Zone of Genius (college advising + 9–12 grade + family and community engagement) to offer one-on-one support and cohort training.

Using the R-E-S framework, she gathered her receipts:

RECEIPTS:

- Led a support initiative that resulted in an increase of 20 percent in graduation rates and 30 percent in college admissions

- Helped her school's seniors in securing over $1.2 million in scholarships in a single academic year

- Increased FAFSA completion rates by 25 percent through targeted workshops for students and families

- Designed and implemented a college readiness program that served 400+ students and families annually
- Helped 70 percent of her first-generation students successfully enroll in four-year colleges
- Coached families through financial aid negotiations that resulted in an average savings of $8,000 per student

EXPERIENCE:

- Master's degree in educational leadership
- High school principal (5 years)
- High school vice principal (3 years)
- High school teacher in speech and English (10 years)
- High school counselor (5 years)

SKILLS:

- College advising expertise: guiding students step-by-step through the college admissions process
- Scholarship research and application support: helping families identify and secure funding opportunities
- Strong verbal and written communication skills

- Program facilitation: designing and leading workshops, trainings, and group sessions
- One-on-one coaching: providing personalized guidance tailored to individual students' goals and needs
- Organizational and project management skills: coordinating multi-step admissions timelines and application requirements
- Data analysis and tracking: monitoring student progress, scholarship outcomes, and admissions results
- Excellent negotiation skills
- Deep understanding of how school leadership must balance broader district concerns and communicate with parents, students, and the community

What I want y'all to notice from Tanisha's example is that your **Receipts** are quantifiable. Maybe it's a statistic that measures improvement as a result of your work, or maybe it's simply a concrete number, like how many students you've worked with, how many teachers you've coached, or how many PD sessions you've led. You get the idea. You want facts and figures.

Experience is a high-level overview of your career, like a résumé, so a good place to start is by looking at your past job experience. When I wrote my own R-E-S, two of my examples are that I have seven years' experience as a school leader and I led weekly PD sessions as a principal. This list is also where you can include some of your professional learning experiences or credentials. If you have certifications or have been through fellowship programs, name those experiences.

Finally, **Skills**. I like to think about this list like the bullet points you might put beneath your job titles on your résumé. For me personally, some examples are building engaging adult-learning experiences, coaching conversations with leaders, and analyzing data at scale. When you define this section, consider what skills you have that relate to the problem you want to solve.

The objective is to help you understand what only you can do, and to make your impact as clear as day. Your R-E-S framework is the foundation for how you're going to talk about what you do. The results, experience, and skills you brainstorm here might appear on your website, or on a one-pager to explain why you're uniquely qualified to do this work. In the future, you might revisit your R-E-S to create marketing content for your personal network or on social media. This isn't busywork; instead, your R-E-S is fundamental to your business.

When you've got a draft that you're happy with, I want you to share it with a friend for a vibe check. Ask them for feedback, including whether you've included all your accomplishments (because high-achieving folks like you and me often forget how many dragons we've slayed). This might seem like an extra step, but it's an important one to make sure that you're not being unnecessarily modest. Educators love to be humble, but humility in entrepreneurship will keep you left out of rooms that you deserve to be in and with pennies in your pocket.

CHAPTER 3 REFLECTION QUESTIONS

1. What is your Zone of Genius, and how does it point you toward the types of problems you're uniquely equipped to solve?

2. Which problem feels so urgent, frustrating, or meaningful to you that working on it makes you "float"?

3. What's your current hypothesis about how to solve the problem you've identified? Make sure you treat this process as an experiment— don't put pressure on yourself to have the "perfect" answer.

4. How can you describe your problem in a way that anyone in your target audience can quickly understand?

ACTION STEPS

- Draft a problem description for your business.
- Draft a problem statement for your business.
- Draft your R-E-S.

7-FIGURE EDUCATOR RESOURCES

Visit **www.7febook.com/resources** to:
- Review sample R-E-S one-pagers

Form Your Framework

Objective: Create a framework for your business

I'm going to say the quiet part out loud.

Your innovation and creativity have been undervalued in the field of education. That's partly because our entire industry sees intellectual property as something to be freely shared in service of the greater good, often at the expense of creators. But let's consider some educators who bucked that expectation.

For example: John G. Sperling, creator of multiple for-profit schools, including the incredibly lucrative University of Phoenix. An early proponent of online education, Sperling wanted to create a university that would accommodate older students who had 9-to-5 jobs. Today, the University of Phoenix—part of a for-profit, publicly traded company—holds more than 30,000 trademarks and a patent for its online course platform. Its parent company is worth more than $84 billion. Forget about being a million-dollar educator—Sperling died a billionaire, and his business helped one million students get degrees from an accredited university.

Here's another example: In the 1850s, a young white man showed up on a Tennessee preacher's farm, looking for work. After sussing out that the boy was a hard worker, the preacher sent him to the distillery on the property to help out with whiskey production. The master distiller at the time was an enslaved Black man named Nathan "Nearest" (sometimes spelled Nearis) Green, who had created his own unique process to distill liquor using charcoal as a filter. At the preacher's request, Green taught the young white man everything he knew. After the Civil War ended in 1865, that young man opened his own distillery, hiring Nearest and two of his sons to help him make whiskey.

That young man was Jack Daniel.

Nathan "Nearest" Green was (mostly) left out of the founding narrative of Jack Daniel's until 2016, when Jack Daniel's Distillery belatedly shared the real truth. A year later, entrepreneur Fawn Weaver officially launched Uncle Nearest Premium Whiskey based on Green's original recipes. Today, the intellectual property of Nathan "Nearest" Green lives on in Jack Daniel's Properties, Inc. (worth approximately $7.1 billion as of 2022) and Uncle Nearest Whiskey (worth approximately $1.1 billion as of 2024 and, to date, the fastest-growing American whiskey brand in history).

I'm sharing these examples so that you can see how ideas translate into ownership, and how ownership can transform into wealth. Let's call up the wisdom of math teachers again and make sure you see the link. If Ideas = Ownership and Ownership = Wealth, then the transitive property says Ideas = Wealth.

It's important to me that you make this connection, because our ancestors didn't have the same opportunities we do today. Consider this. Even though Nearest Green was legally eligible to apply for patents and trademarks for his unique approach to making whiskey, as a formerly enslaved man in the 1800s, he likely would not have known those protections were available to him. And even if he had known about those protections, he would have faced significant barriers to getting them.

Today we have both the knowledge and the access to control the ownership of our ideas. Remember, anything you create from your own genius counts as intellectual property. Even if you're using research to inform your work, how you approach your work, or create your strategy, or the framework you build based on all those things is entirely your own. Going back to Uncle Nearest Whiskey, the recipe the company uses is their intellectual property. Their branding, the type of mash and how long they distill, even the shape of their bottles—all of that is their intellectual property. Because that's what makes them unique, that's what makes them different, even from Jack Daniel's and its shared origins. Your intellectual property is your special sauce that makes you and what you sell solely yours. Use the story of Nearest Green as an easy way to remember why you're creating a framework in the first place. To outline the recipe, to show off the special sauce that makes you and what you sell unique.

I want to share one final note about the intersection between intellectual property, the framework you're about to create, and the broader goals of this book. Your framework is a wealth-building tool because it positions you for later conversations around licensing your intellectual property to others. Let's say that a few years from now, you have a client that is part of an organization, a school, or even a whole district that says something like, "Hey, we love the work that you're doing so much. We would love to have access to your curriculum and make it part of what we do." When you give them permission to use your trademarked and copyrighted content in exchange for getting paid, that's licensing. There are all sorts of ways to do this, but licensing can allow you to get paid without having to do more work. (Jumping back to the seven-streams-of-income conversation from Chapter 3, this is an example of a passive revenue stream for your business.)

You aren't able to access this benefit without a framework. Think of your framework as the recipe to your special sauce. It's replicable. Back when I first started helping educators who wanted to be entrepreneurs, I had to show up to every single one of those one-on-one conversations to get paid. However, once I had developed a framework, I could organize all those conversations into a digital course that I had to deliver and record only once. My digital course continued to help educators, but I could be hands-off while still generating revenue for my business.

I cannot stress enough the value and importance of developing your framework as a foundational piece of intellectual property. In addition to being a helpful cheat code to stay focused on the problem only you can solve, the framework and everything else you create within your business are also assets that build wealth.

DEFINING A FRAMEWORK

As a high school math teacher in Charlotte, North Carolina, I knew my standards by heart. I remember receiving the district's pacing guide that outlined recommended units and the order in which I should teach them. But teacher Ms. JT still had to do the heavy lifting of breaking down those standards into unit assessments, daily objectives, and daily lesson plans.

Having defined standards around what my students needed to learn allowed me, as well as every other geometry teacher in my building and district, to backwards plan. Curriculum standards define parameters of what is on grade level and what is not and give us a focused pathway to our desired outcomes. From there, teachers can design lesson plans and assessments to meet or exceed those standards within a school year. Within education more broadly, standards serve as checks and balances to ensure every student across a district, state, and even the whole country are at-minimum proficient in foundational skills.

As you might have already discovered, entrepreneurship doesn't have content standards to define what is "on or off grade level" in your business. Instead, we get to create these standards for ourselves. Your standards are your framework, a valuable piece of intellectual property that's going to help you build ownership in your business and provide the foundation for future creativity, innovation, and wealth.

Now that you have your problem defined, I'm going to help you craft a framework that you can use to explain at a high level what your business does and how it does it. (Here's a meta moment. Do you see that learning arch I've got from chapter to chapter? The educator in me is showing out!) I'm also going to help you understand exactly how using a framework can work as a cheat code to marketing and delivering your services. I'll explain what a framework is and what it ain't, and share lots of examples. Last, I'll walk you step-by-step through the process of creating your own unique framework.

Let's dig in.

What a framework is ... and is not

For our purposes, a framework is a system that outlines how your business solves the one problem you defined in Chapter 3. Like educational standards, a framework provides structure, direction, and focus. It defines your content lane so you can stay focused as a business. It outlines at a high level your business's methodology, but it doesn't get so specific that it defines your services. Having a framework allows you to determine your topics for content, your offers, and your marketing messages. A framework is a blueprint, not a definition. Frameworks are flexible. What you create today is meant to evolve as you learn and grow.

FRAMEWORKS AS CHEAT CODES

The very first offer I ever created in my coaching business was one-on-one strategy sessions with educators. I did roughly 25 of these sessions before I realized two things. First, everyone asked the same questions. Second, I could serve more people, more efficiently, by offering a group-coaching program. But when I launched that group program, I realized that people were *still* asking the same questions and still struggling because they didn't know how to *apply* what they were learning. What my clients needed was a system that translated the answers to their questions into action steps. That system became a framework, which—spoiler alert— is the foundation of my coaching program and ultimately this book.

I first learned about frameworks when I was in a large group-coaching cohort where a business coach was teaching us the basics. Many of my fellow entrepreneurs were confused, because most had never really seen a framework before. But I was already familiar. You are too. While educators might not use the term *framework*, this method of communicating a system is *everywhere* in education. Common Core is a great example. No matter the district, no matter the city, no matter the state, there are a set of defined standards for every core subject and every grade level. Common Core is a framework that millions of teachers and administrators across the U.S. rely on and use in the classroom year after year.

As entrepreneurs, we can develop similar systems for ourselves. We can create content standards for what we teach and what we don't, the results your business provides, and how it provides them. Like standards in the classroom, creating a framework for your business starts with the outcome that your service provides and what you teach to your client/students in order to achieve that outcome. By doing so, your framework narrows your focus into a single subject that you teach (the one problem you solve) and even the specific "grade level" you serve (your target audience). Work backward from your framework to create offers, messaging, and more to attract the audience that wants your results (which I'll help you work on later in the book).

Your framework allows you to know exactly when you're in your lane and when you're stepping out. An important lesson to learn in entrepreneurship is that our businesses need boundaries just like our classrooms do. A framework puts those boundaries in place. At some point you might purposely choose to do work that's outside your framework. But that choice will be intentional, because your framework has given you clear, defined boundaries around what you say yes to. (And in turn, what you don't.) Having a framework avoids the biggest mistake that new entrepreneurs make, which is not having a clear-enough focus. Taking on a little of this and a little of that, letting what other people want to hire and pay you for drive your business rather than what you can uniquely do best. That approach will have you gone with the wind but not fabulous. It'll prevent you from being able to grow and scale quickly, and, ultimately, from being able to generate wealth and create an impact that lasts.

FRAMEWORKS FROM EDUCATION

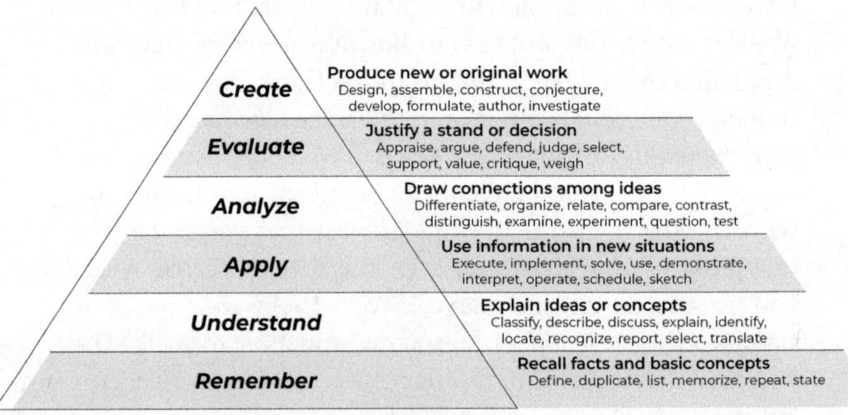

BLOOM'S TAXONOMY

As I mentioned before, educators use frameworks for damn near everything. A great example is Bloom's Taxonomy for learning, which you were probably introduced to in your early years as an educator. Developed in the 1950s, this framework categorizes educational goals, objectives, and skills that teachers can utilize to create effective instruction. Looking at the pyramid chart, it's easy to see how the framework is structured. The first learning skill—the foundation—is recalling information (remember), and the last is generating original work in response to what's being taught (create). Something I want you to notice is that Bloom's Taxonomy doesn't tell you *what* you'll be doing or *how* you'll be achieving these goals. In other words, it doesn't name activities.

Frameworks aren't focused on the "what" or the "how." They don't spell out your services or teaching objectives. Instead, your framework reveals your broader approach. Bloom's Taxonomy is a framework for instructional design. It doesn't prescribe a service—like a semester-long PD series or a 90-day online course—it outlines the methodology for deepening learning, moving from recall to higher-order thinking like analysis and evaluation. The service model to accomplish the goal of deeper learning is flexible, but the framework stays the same. Your framework is your methodology for reaching your goal; your services are the vehicles for delivering it.

Let's consider another tool: the McREL Framework. In case you're not familiar, this is a teacher-evaluation tool. Think a simplified version of the Danielson Framework (another framework!).

MCREL FRAMEWORK

Standard 1:   Teachers demonstrate leadership.

Standard 2:   Teachers establish a respectful environment for a diverse population of students.

Standard 3:   Teachers know the content they teach.

Standard 4:   Teachers facilitate learning for their students.

Standard 5:   Teachers reflect on their practice.

You'll notice that, once again, this framework doesn't tell us the services that McREL International provides to schools and districts. There aren't any specific objectives around *what* to do or *how* to accomplish these standards. The "how" is what you pay for when you hire the company to help your district evaluate teachers.

Last, I want to share my own framework for the business coaching we do with our clients launching their education consulting business.

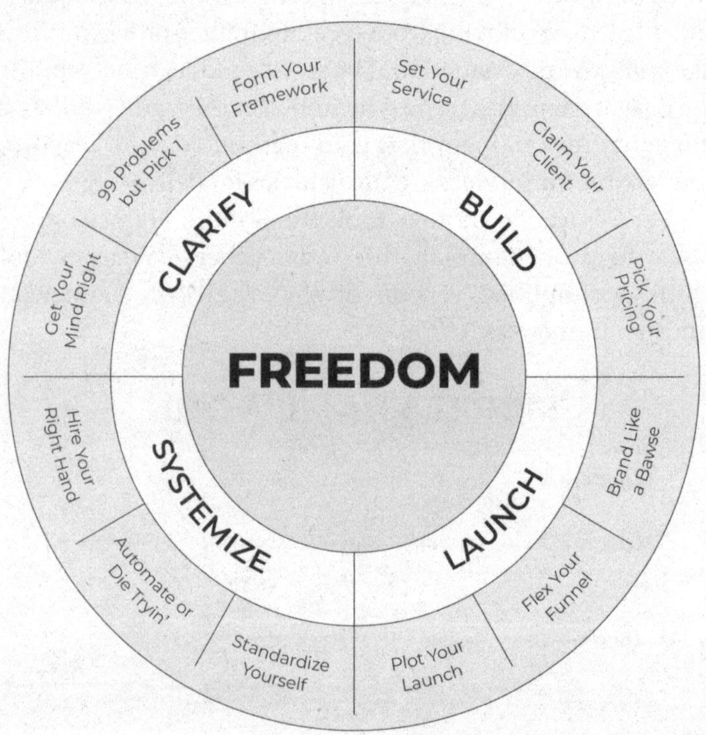

As you can see, there's no one set way a framework has to look. There are as many frameworks as there are businesses, but these examples should give you some ideas to get started.

THE THREE COMPONENTS OF YOUR FRAMEWORK

Let's revisit the analogy that your framework is like education standards for your business. Whatever you teach, whether that is third-grade math or seventh-grade ELA or high school chemistry, you have a set of standards. But those standards don't tell you *how* to teach that particular class or subject. The standards don't outline lesson plans. Sometimes they don't even list specific objectives. Instead, those standards are meant to give you guidance and direction. That's the same for your framework. It's meant to provide structure, direction, and guidance for your business. And, similar to the standards you had when you were a teacher, what's there is a little loose.

As I pointed out in the examples, your framework does not define how you're going to do the work, or the services you're gonna offer. The objective of a framework is to give you direction while also creating space for you to evolve in your offers and even your methodology.

Building your framework can seem like a gargantuan task, but I'm going to help you step-by-step. Remember, your framework doesn't have to be pulled entirely from your brain and your own career. While your framework does come from your own experience, it can also be informed by research, by theory, by practice. The important thing is that the framework you come up with is unique to you and your business.

There are three parts to your framework:
- Theme
- Concepts
- Client Objectives

Because we're all educators, you know I'm going to make analogies to what you already know to help codify your learning. I'm also going to break this down two ways. First, I'm going to explain these concepts from the top down so you understand what you're doing. Then I'll show you how to build your framework from the bottom up using the work you did in Chapter 3. The reason I teach frameworks this way is because it helps you understand what you're about to do and then shows you how to reverse engineer that 'ish.

So, let's start at the top, the highest level of your framework: the **Theme.**

One helpful way to think of this is like a unit theme. Back in the day when I was a geometry teacher, one of my unit themes was "Similarities & Right Triangles." While there were multiple curriculum standards and daily objectives within that theme, teaching my students to understand similarities and properties of right triangles was the higher-level focus. Bringing the analogy back to your business, your framework will have a similar overarching theme. Your theme is your big message, maybe your motto or mantra, that describes the overall result you deliver to clients.

The next level down from your Theme are your **Concepts**.

Jumping back to my time as a geometry teacher, each unit grouped similar standards. For example, within my unit of Similarities & Right Triangles, there would be standards of determining if two triangles are similar, solving problems using similarity criteria that my students needed to be proficient in when I was done teaching that unit. You want to make sure that you don't overdo this part of your framework. A good rule of thumb is to limit your concepts to three, maybe five at most.

Your concepts come from a broader list of actions called **Client Objectives**.

This is the most nitty-gritty, nuanced level. This is where your daily objectives and lesson plans live. This is where you are defining the skills and outcomes that will be built through your services. I promise that this will make more sense after we start cookin' and build your framework. Remember too that there's lots of different ways to package your framework. You get to pick whatever structure feeds and fits your soul. The important thing is to get clear on the core components of your framework, knowing that the perfect design to showcase your genius will show up later.

BUILDING YOUR FRAMEWORK

If Michael Jordan had to come up with a framework for how to play basketball—he might be stumped. He might actually say something like, "I don't know how to explain it to you, 'cause, chile, I just do it." Identifying what makes his game magical might be challenging for MJ because he probably doesn't have to think about what he's doing. That's the beauty of being in your Zone of Genius—of finding that space where you float. You're so good, you don't even really know how to explain how you're floating and making things happen. You just are.

I say that because I'm going to ask you to think about *how* you float.

How you do what you do. *How* you become magical.

Making what's unconscious conscious might be challenging, so give yourself grace and the space to iterate. Creating your framework is asking you to put words to things that you've likely been doing for a long time without really thinking about it. You're probably going to go through multiple revisions. You may want to ask a trusted friend or colleague for feedback and maybe go through a couple of feedback loops for your framework to feel right. That's okay and to be expected. For this work and generally throughout this book: Trust that when you feel challenged by the work, you're doing it right.

Let's start building your framework by identifying the finer details of what you do: your Client Objectives.

STEP 1: DEFINE YOUR CLIENT OBJECTIVES

Begin this work by carefully rereading your problem statement and description. Make a list of the steps it would take to meaningfully solve the problem you identify in your problem statement and description. Be as generative as possible. You don't need the steps to be sequential unless that helps you, but be sure you cover the whole journey from problem to solution—every single step.

Let's use the problem statement and description I shared in Chapter 3 from my consulting business as an example:

> Sixty-seven percent of principals agree that typical leadership programs and graduate schools of education are out of touch with the realities of what it takes to run today's school districts.

> The average principal is hired into their role underprepared, handed the keys to their building, and expected to lead with little onboarding or

support. Today's principals are overwhelmed by the responsibilities of the role and lack access to quality professional development. If this problem persists, principals will continue to leave their schools after three years, and our schools will continue to struggle in meeting the needs of all students. **The problem my business is solving is the gap in quality principal professional development**.

Given my own problem statement, I would list out all the steps that a principal would have to take in order for them to be an effective leader for their school. I would ask myself, What tasks would a principal have to master? The quick list I came up with includes: time management, instructional coaching, staff culture, student culture, analyzing data, family and community engagement, strategic planning, monitoring systems, building assessment systems, setting vision, leading professional development, giving feedback, and managing district relationships.

Note that I'm writing these as topics rather than as objectives. The goal is to have 6 to 10 objectives, but if you have more or fewer than that—it's okay. Creating your framework is not pass-fail or really graded at all. Instead, the goal is to continually refine what you have until it works for the current version of your business. Once you do have a list of client objectives that you're satisfied with, you can move on to the next step.

STEP 2: IDENTIFY YOUR CONCEPTS

Take a look at your client objectives and ask yourself: What are the underlying concepts within them? Going back to my list, I see that a lot of my client objectives are related and could be grouped into three broader concepts of leadership:

- Instructional Leadership: instructional coaching, building assessment systems, leading professional development, and giving feedback;

- Strategic Leadership: time management, analyzing data, strategic planning, monitoring systems, and setting vision; and

- Cultural Leadership: staff culture, student culture, family and community engagement, managing district relationships.

The goal is to land on three to five concepts so that your framework remains focused. Once you have those, move on to the third and final step.

STEP 3: FIND YOUR THEME

I want you to consider this prompt: In one to three words, describe the overall result that you will deliver to your client. In other words, what's the headline of these concepts? What's your mantra? What's the North Star? In my own example, I could use the words *prepare* or *achieve*, or the most obvious: *lead*. There are lots of options for me, and likely for you too.

Brainstorm. Going back to our earlier analogy to unit themes, what would the title of this unit be if you were teaching it in a classroom?

After generating my client objectives, concepts, and themes, I came up with the PreparED Principal Framework.

PREPARED PRINCIPAL FRAMEWORK

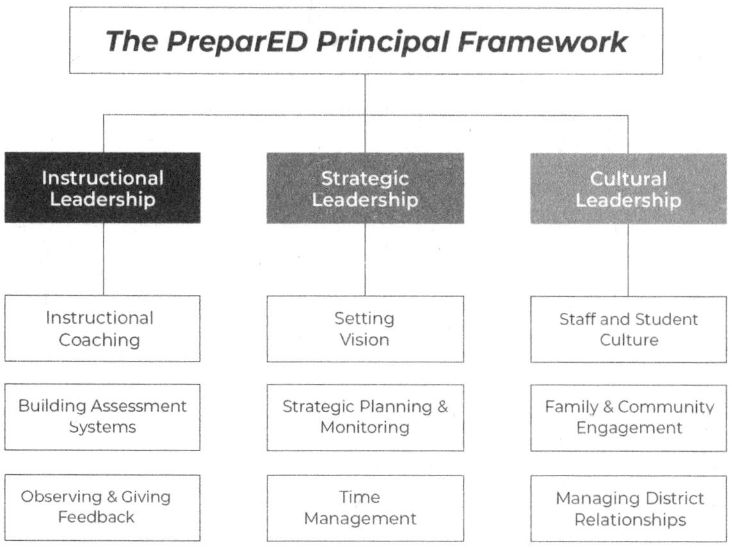

Remember: The design of your framework doesn't have to look like mine. But let's review it. The three components are there, and they are:

Theme:

PreparED Principal ✔

Concepts:

Instructional Leadership ✔

Strategic Leadership ✔

Cultural Leadership ✔

Remember, the goal is to have three (and definitely no more than five), because we want our framework to be focused. Ultimately these three concepts should be easy to remember and repeat even when your framework isn't right in front of you. Concepts should be core to your business.

Client Objectives:

Instructional coaching, building assessment systems, and observing and giving feedback are the three points under Instructional Leadership. ✓

Setting vision, strategic planning and monitoring, and time management are the three pieces under Strategic Leadership. ✓

Staff and student culture, family and community engagement, and managing district relationships are under Cultural Leadership. ✓

Notice that nothing here tells me what services are being offered. While the framework gives me focus and direction—I can teach on any of the nine objectives I've outlined—it doesn't specifically say I do this or I do that. For example, let's say that I get requests from various district administrators asking for principal professional development help. With my framework, I could offer any number of services to meet those needs. I could do a single presentation on my PreparED Principal theme, or I could do a series of PD workshops based on my three leadership concepts, or I could do one-on-one coaching with individual principals on any one of my nine client objectives. There are lots of options here, and what I want you to see is that my framework remains flexible even though I've clearly defined the problem I solve and the ways in which I can solve it.

Your framework is going to be your anchor throughout the rest of the book, and really through all the versions of your business as it evolves. Again, I want to remind you that this is meant to be iterative. Your framework is meant to flex as you do. The task right now is to think through your client objectives, your concepts, and your theme so that you can build the first version of your framework from the bottom up.

A note on framework models, designs, and structures

There is no single framework model.

People use all sorts of visual templates for their frameworks: pyramids, flow charts, Venn diagrams—or, like with McREL, no chart at all. While templates can be helpful (and there are plenty available in the online resources for this book), it's important to give yourself permission to use what works for you. In my experience, templates can cause more problems than they solve, because they limit you to the template's boundaries. In reality, there are no boundaries outside of what you yourself create.

You do have to create them, though. In fact, that's the only real "rule" when it comes to creating your framework. You want to make sure you don't outline a dozen themes and 50 core objectives, because that will defeat the purpose of your framework, which is to give guidance and direction. The words matter more than what shape they take. I've seen people get tripped up focusing on making their ideas fit a certain design aesthetic or chart template, but, ultimately, whether your framework ends up as a circle or a PowerPoint slide doesn't really matter that much.

What matters, instead, is that your framework feels personal, fits the needs of your business, and encapsulates your Zone of Genius. Give yourself permission to iterate, to refine, and to create in whatever way feels most meaningful for you. I promise that you'll land on a framework that *works* in the end.

CHAPTER 4 REFLECTION QUESTIONS

1. What patterns, steps, or processes do you consistently use with clients that could form the foundation of your own framework?

2. How does your lived experience as an educator shape the unique perspective your framework brings to solving problems?

3. In what ways could naming and documenting your framework increase your credibility, authority, and ownership in your field?

4. How does thinking of your framework as intellectual property shift the way you see its value in your business?

5. If someone tried to copy your work tomorrow, what about your framework would make it unmistakably yours?

ACTION STEPS

- Develop a rough framework for your business, and check your work:

  - Does your framework have a theme of 1 to 3 words that match the outcomes you can deliver and the concepts you've listed?

  - Does your framework have 3 to 5 core concepts?

  - Does your framework have 6 to 10 client objectives that fit within your concepts?

- Does your framework have consistent language (i.e., are concepts and objectives listed as all verbs or all nouns)?

- Does your framework feel like you? Have you added your own personality and swag?

7-FIGURE EDUCATOR RESOURCES

Visit **www.7febook.com/resources** to:

- Download sample framework templates

PART II

Build

CHAPTER 5

Set Your Service

Objective: Define your service model and tiered offers

Greg had a successful consulting business that was earning ~$600,000 in annual revenue. He sold coaching packages that included a quarterly in-person day, a monthly group-coaching call, and a biweekly one-on-one advisory call with individual educators. Like many entrepreneurs, Greg's goal was to grow his business to seven figures and beyond. But he couldn't get there. While his business was profitable and his customer demand grew quickly, Greg was stuck because the offer he had created simply wasn't scalable.

Greg is not alone. What I see in my community of educators-turned-entrepreneurs is that people often start with offers and business models that aren't scalable to start with. Sometimes, it's because they feel nervous about pricing, like Greg did, and offer lots of time-intensive bells and whistles. I am talkin' the entire kitchen sink. Other times, entrepreneurs start with a too-low-priced offer like an e-book without a big-enough audience or enough customer demand to make it profitable.

In this chapter I'm going to teach you how to avoid these mistakes by helping you understand all the service models that are available to you so that you can pick something that is scalable right from the jump. To begin, let's talk about what *scalable* means. By my definition, scaling is when your service model allows you to grow the number of clients you serve and the money you bring in *without increasing expenses*. That's different from when you're in building mode—where you're experimenting to see what works—or when you're in growth mode and your expenses are going up right alongside your client list and your overall revenue.

Here's a quick example. Let's say that like Greg, you have an offer that includes one-on-one coaching. Within that service model, when you have more clients, you need more coaches. So, that offer is not scalable, because as the number of clients you serve grows, so do your expenses. However, if you instead decide to offer an online course, that model *would* be scalable, because there's no limit to how many people you could enroll in that course and the majority of your expenses are one-time up-front costs for development and launch. So, even when your course has 10 times or 100 times the number of people initially enrolled, your costs remain the same while your profit and revenue rise.

Here is what I want to make sure you don't miss: Building a business model around a scalable offer is how you build wealth in entrepreneurship—because you are no longer exchanging time for money. Landing on what that model *is* may include some experimentation. You might not be able to know what your target client needs from you until you work with them. You may need to start off charging by the hour to understand the value (both monetary and otherwise) of your offers in order to transition to charging a flat rate. Going back to Robert Kiyosaki's four quadrants that I mentioned in

Chapter 2, the goal is ownership of a business and of systems that create a result rather than owning a job where you are putting in hours in exchange for getting paid.

As educators, we've been taught to define value as being physically present. When we work in schools—even though we never officially clock in or out—we don't get paid if we're not physically there. As a teacher, I was a 10-month employee, which meant when school was out for the summer, I didn't get paid. This may be why the educational consulting world also defaults to highly personalized, custom, time-intensive solutions. In the end, that conditioning influenced Greg. To charge what he wanted to charge ($50,000), he felt like he *had* to include a school visit and multiple coaching calls in his coaching package. But the real value of Greg's work was the transformation he provided for people and how quickly he delivered that change. When he was able to embrace that truth, Greg was able to scale his coaching package down to what his clients really needed—and make his business scalable too.

What Greg experienced is typical for educators just starting their consulting business. Most people begin with what they're familiar with, which usually reflects the services we received ourselves as educators—professional development (PD) or one-on-one coaching. But, like Greg, most of the time, the first offers you create aren't going to be what you continue with. Even with the best advice possible—which you're gonna get in this chapter—you aren't going to land on the perfect set of offers the first time you try.

If you were the type of educator who always had a perfectly detailed and executed lesson plan with multicolored highlighter pens, this might be hard for you to hear. Up to this moment, you have likely been successful because you have always done the most. You have worked twice as hard, crossing all the *t*'s and dotting every single *i*, never caught slippin'. Most educators I know are used to knowing the answer, creating a plan around the answer, and executing that plan. Entrepreneurship does not work this way. Most of the time, you don't know the answer—it isn't found in a book or academic journal or podcast; it's found by running an experiment to test your idea and making an informed decision based on the results. Not knowing the answer can feel frustrating. If you're feeling that way right now reading this, I see you. Because I *was* you. Lean into that discomfort—because, like we tell our students, if you are uncomfortable, that means you are growing.

Know that success *will* arrive when you land on the right combination of offers for you *and* for the clients you serve. That's a delicate balance that reveals itself over time. In the meantime, we can experiment and still earn money. With that frame in mind, I'm setting a bold intention for this chapter to help you move forward. I am going to ask that you shift your focus from creating the perfect offer (and business) to generating revenue. Specifically, your goal will be to generate money in the next 30 days from a scalable offer you create using the advice in this chapter.

To help you, I'm going to outline nine services that you can use to deliver solutions to the problem you identified in Chapter 3. Keep in mind that some of these services require months of planning and pre-work. And while you can certainly aspire to use these service models in the future, the objective of this chapter isn't to kick off three to six months of planning while you're earning zero dollars. We don't roll like that.

Instead, you will choose a couple service models to experiment with based on your individual strengths. From there, I'll explain my 7-FigurED Offer framework, which creates a tiered structure of offers that allows you to work with clients at different price points as well as upsell and downsell when appropriate, and encourages repeat customers. By the end of this chapter, you'll be familiar with all the options you have to serve your target audience and be ready to experiment with an offer that brings in cash.

SERVICE MODELS

The first step to creating structure within your business is to choose a service model: *how* you are going to deliver your services, *how* you solve your client's problem. As usual, there's no "right" or "wrong" service model. Instead, there's only the right and wrong service model for you. I'm going to outline nine different service models. Remember, the goal isn't to use every single model or even start with where you aim to finish. Instead, consider what you can take action on today to start your experiment and generate revenue in the next 30 days. Consider what service model(s) fit your strengths, complement your R-E-S, and work with the problem you're solving in your business. Remember too that entrepreneurship is a journey of growth and experimentation. If a service model appeals to you, go ahead and try that 'ish. You really have nothing to lose, and so much learning (and revenue) to gain.

1. Professional Development/Trainings

The most common offer in education is consulting. Professional development (PD) is an online or in-person experience designed to teach a skill and/or knowledge to professional educators. Typically, PD is delivered either in half-day or full-day sessions. While requirements vary from state to state, in the U.S. all teachers are required to participate in professional development or continuing education to keep their licenses. Because of that requirement, PD is both in high demand and has a high potential for recurring revenue from repeat customers. Another benefit to PD is that how you structure your sessions is up to you. You can do one-time PD sessions, structure PD packages, or offer a PD series. Because you are often presenting to groups of people within a school district, a city, and/or at a conference, there is high potential to both convert existing clients beyond a one-time delivery and attract new clients with every PD you teach.

However, offering PD requires significant prep time. In a lot of ways, PD is like teaching in a classroom. You need to create a lesson plan and be clear on your materials, your objective, and your delivery. Another downside is that most of the time, school districts pay after services are rendered, meaning that you won't get paid until you deliver the PD. That can mean that you likely need to pay up front for costs like travel and materials.

2. One-on-One Coaching

Familiar to most educators, this service model is where you support individual clients in reaching their goals through coaching. A big benefit to starting your business with one-on-one coaching is that you can learn a lot about each and every client you work with while getting paid. Early in my own business, I found that offering paid consultations was a great way to serve my target audience while also being able to do market research. Not only did I notice trends and patterns in the questions people asked, but I was also able to test my framework as a viable solution in each of those con-versations. That allowed me to tweak my framework to better fit the problem my target audience was experiencing and how I could help solve it.

Similarly, the deep connections that one-on-one coaching requires can allow you to get huge results and glowing testimonials from the clients you work with, which then benefit you as your business grows. Starting your business by offering one-on-one coaching is also fast and simple, because all you need is a scheduling tool to set up appointments and a system for following up. Individualized coaching is also flexible, because you can decide to offer it as a one-time consultation or as an ongoing commitment with a specific start and end date.

The big downside of this service model, however, is that it's not scalable since you are directly exchanging time for money.

3. Online Course

There's a lot of variation within the online learning world, but for our purposes, an online course is guided but asynchronous. Meaning that you must design, build, present, and record the course, but then you can market and sell it forever, because clients can access the recordings whenever they'd like. The biggest advantage to this service model is that you have to deliver the content only once. Because the number of people who could enroll in your course is unlimited (especially compared to other business models I've mentioned, like PD and one-on-one coaching), there is high revenue potential without increased cost.

That said, building a successful online course requires a lot of work up front. You have to develop and organize your content, do a lot of beta testing with your target audience, create any additional materials like slides and handouts, record the content, and upload the content to a learning-management platform. Also, online courses are best paired with a community strategy, meaning that it's best practice to create and manage a virtual community for enrollees of the course. That could be a private Facebook group, a Slack channel, or using a learning-management platform that offers virtual community features. You also have to market the course effectively and nearly continually to get people to buy. The amount of work is similar to creating an entire curriculum from scratch, which is why I advise people to *grow into* an online course rather than starting there.

4. Group Coaching

This service model is simple. You provide coaching and support to a small group (5 to 12 people) who have a similar need. Most group-coaching programs are 6 to 12 weeks long. The biggest advantages to this service model are that you can generate impact with multiple clients at the same time and you can create community by gathering people with similar problems together. In a lot of ways, group coaching is a hybrid of one-on-one coaching and PD. In group-coaching programs, you will typically present the content in live sessions (either virtual or in person), which is great preparation and testing ground for future online courses. Like online courses, most group-coaching programs also include a community element like a Facebook group.

The big downside to group coaching is that you need to enroll a group of people rather than individual clients. That requires an intentional sales strategy and usually a significant investment of time or money to enroll the number of people you want. (I've personally found the sweet spot to be 8 to 10 people.) Similarly, you also have to create and maintain a community for 6 to 12 weeks and show up regularly to support your clients. That community could be in a private Facebook group, a Slack channel, or another similar software, but it requires you to create expectations and culture for the group while folks are participating, and for you to be engaged and responsive in the community.

5. Membership Community

This is a paid-subscription community that provides a variety of ongoing services and support for people with similar needs and problems. So, I want you to think Netflix; I want you to think Hulu; I want you to think Planet Fitness. These are all subscription models where we pay a monthly fee in exchange for access to services. The biggest advantage to this service model is that you create monthly recurring revenue—you know a certain amount of money is coming in every month no matter what.

That said, maintaining a membership community can require a lot of ongoing work, and the value needs to be clear. What can members expect? For example, a membership community I belonged to included access to an online course, monthly Q&A calls, and a Slack community where we could ask questions anytime and get answers within 24 business hours. What you include as part of your membership is completely up to you, but the details must be clear in order to get people to enroll and stay enrolled. The big challenge to maintaining a membership community long term is that you have to simultaneously strategically market to potential new members while delivering high-quality content and value to existing ones. That requires you to plan ahead and communicate clearly what's coming up over the next three to six months so that you can get your current clients to stick.

Last, most of the time, membership communities are a high-volume model, meaning that you must attract a lot of members in order to be profitable. Given that memberships range from $10 to $300 per month, you can see that you would need anywhere from 33 to 1,000 active members in order to generate $10,000 in monthly recurring revenue. Like online courses, a membership community may be an offer you grow into later on in your business.

6. Speaking Engagements

Let me be clear: *Paid* speaking engagements are a service model, whereas speaking engagements you do for *free* are marketing.

Don't get me wrong—I'm not saying you shouldn't do free speaking engagements. You can, especially in the early stages of your business. They're a great marketing opportunity to spread the word about your new business and what you do. But moving to *paid* speaking engagements changes the game. In addition to spreading the word about your business and how amazing you are, you're earning revenue. When you start getting paid to speak, you can develop a signature talk that you can reuse over and over (and over). You could have one signature talk or three or even five. Once you have proven content, the prep time for each engagement decreases until eventually you can tweak your talk for any specific audience with ease. The expenses associated with speaking engagements are mostly travel (if the speaking engagement is in person), and the time and brainpower it takes to prep and write your speech.

That said, the downside to paid speaking engagements as a service model is that most provide one-time revenue unless you include it with other offers like PD or coaching. That's why many of the educators I work with offer paid speaking as one of the services they offer but not the primary service. Similarly, at some speaking engagements (like conferences), you aren't able to pitch from the stage, meaning that you can't present a call to action for the audience to work with you again. And, like all the service models, booking paid speaking requires strategic marketing—including making yourself known as *the* go-to expert on the problem your business solves.

7. Project-Based Engagements

This service model consists of time-bound or outcome-driven client projects with specific objectives. Common examples include: building a curriculum for a client, building a leadership development program for a client, or taking on a time-bound project for a district, a school, an organization, or even an individual educator.

An advantage of this service model is that it provides long-term revenue, because most projects require lengthy contracts. This model also allows you to go really deep in your expertise and flex the knowledge you have of the problem you're solving for your client. Because of this, your project-based engagements need to be priced appropriately in acknowledgment of the fact that your genius and intellectual property are at the core of what you're offering.

With project-based engagements, it's really important to clarify intellectual property rights and the scope of work you're agreeing to. The common expectation when you create something on behalf of a client is that ownership transfers from you to the client in exchange for the money you're being paid. That said, each individual situation is different, and you want to review every contract you sign to ensure you understand what you are truly agreeing to.

A big downside to project-based engagements is that most require a formal "request for proposal" or RFP, which means that you have to invest time up front before even being approved for the project, much less paid. That can be risky for obvious reasons, especially when you're first getting started.

Another drawback of this service model is that most project-based engagements are limited to single projects without the potential for recurring revenue or repeat customers. That said, there is always an opportunity to be creative and combine a project-based engagement with complementary services like PD or coaching. Project-based engagements can be a great service model to start with, because there's high potential for revenue among your existing network with no significant prep work or financial investment.

8. VIP Days/Intensives

Popular in online entrepreneurship, VIP days are single-day intensives (either virtual or in person) focused on a specific outcome or deliverable. Most of the time, VIP days are one-on-one but can be expanded for a small group (think teachers for the same grade level at the same school). This service model is uncommon in education consulting, so I'd like to give you an example. Let's say your business is focused on teaching school leaders how to deliver effective professional development for their teachers. You might have a VIP day where you spend six hours with a client and by the end of those six hours, they leave with their PD calendar for the next school year along with plans for coaching and follow-up with individual teachers at their school. The idea is that during the VIP day, you are focused on one or two outcomes or deliverables so that the client leaves with everything they need to execute on a larger goal.

Like one-on-one coaching, VIP days provide a lot of insight into your target client because you're spending so much deep, intimate time together. VIP days also require less time than other service models, both in preparation and delivery. While you do have to make an effort beforehand

and have a process to tailor the VIP experience to each client's needs, the one-on-one work is done in one day.

Remember, when we say VIP day, we're not just slapping *VIP* on it because it sounds good. A VIP day *is* a VIP experience, so you must be extra with the details. For virtual VIP days, you could send flowers or personalized thank-you cards or even a gift in advance of the big day. Often when VIP days are done in person, the "host" covers the costs of the day, including meals, a co-working space, even the client's transportation to and from the meeting space. Often, VIP days include support or follow-up afterward, either through a short consultation call or e-mail.

While VIP days do require planning and individualization, this service model has high revenue potential because the price point is at least four figures (virtual) to five figures (in person). Like one-on-one coaching, you can offer this as a separate service or make this the basis of your business where you host three to four VIP days every month. VIP days can be an efficient way to manage your time and create flexibility in your business while generating results and revenue.

Use your strengths

Understanding what service model is going to work best for you requires you to know yourself well. That's why I recommend you invest in a proven leadership assessment like Gallup CliftonStrengths to identify what your natural strengths are.

For example, according to that assessment, my number one strength is "Relator"—being able to form deep and close relationships one-on-one. That's why I feel like I'm floating when I'm working with individual clients. My strengths also lie in influencing and executing. That means I naturally speak up, take charge, and am able to motivate others (influencing) while getting work done and making things happen (executing). When I first started my business, I considered all those strengths when picking out service models and offers to experiment with.

Keep in mind, your strengths don't have to dictate what you do. I may be great at building relationships, but that doesn't mean my service model needs to be one-on-one coaching. However, I might embed an element of that into a range of services that capitalize on everything else I'm good at. For example, perhaps I use my executing and relationship skills in a VIP day or use my influencing skills to land PD contracts with one-on-one coaching as an add-on. The objective is to remember your strengths and to incorporate those into what you're offering so that you land in your Zone of Genius.

THE 7-FIGURED OFFER FRAMEWORK

Now that you're familiar with service models, it's time to experiment with structuring what you'll offer your customers. Before we dive in, let's check your goals. While the long-term goal is to have offers that attract your target audience and make you millions, the immediate goal is to experiment with ways to bring in revenue within 30 days. You want to focus on the offer and service model that's possible to launch and to earn money from today.

How you're going to structure your offers is similar to how you respond in the classroom when a student is struggling. Specifically with Response to Intervention (RTI).

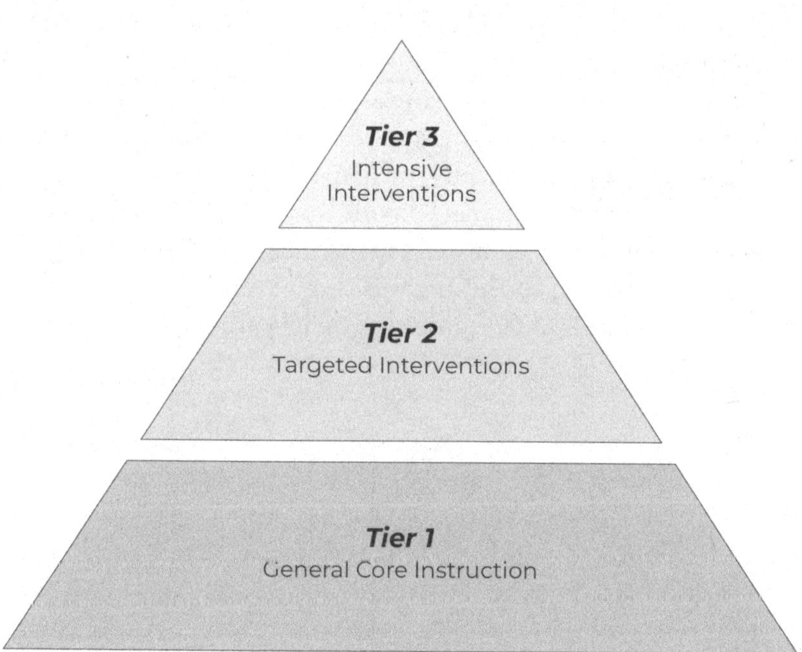

The RTI framework offers three levels of interventions to help students. The bottom level, Tier 1, helps the largest number of students while offering the least individualized attention. The type of curriculum that is taught school-wide is an example of a Tier 1 intervention—high impact and also impacts a large number of students. The middle level, Tier 2, is a set of targeted interventions for small groups. Often this shows up as a small group of students pulled out of their general education classroom for specialized instruction. The top level, Tier 3, is intensive and individualized help. Today, this commonly shows up as an Individualized Education Program (IEP) crafted for a single student. Since it was widely adopted in 2004, RTI has helped educators identify students who are struggling sooner and rapidly implement changes and interventions that help avoid gaps in learning. The success of this framework has been attributed to how easy it is to understand and implement.

Businesses have been using a similar strategy with offers and pricing for decades. Using a tiered structure of offers where the price is directly related to the level of service ensures a better customer experience while also boosting sales and customer retention. This approach works incredibly well for education consulting, which is why it's also the basis for the 7-FigurED Offer framework we'll be using.

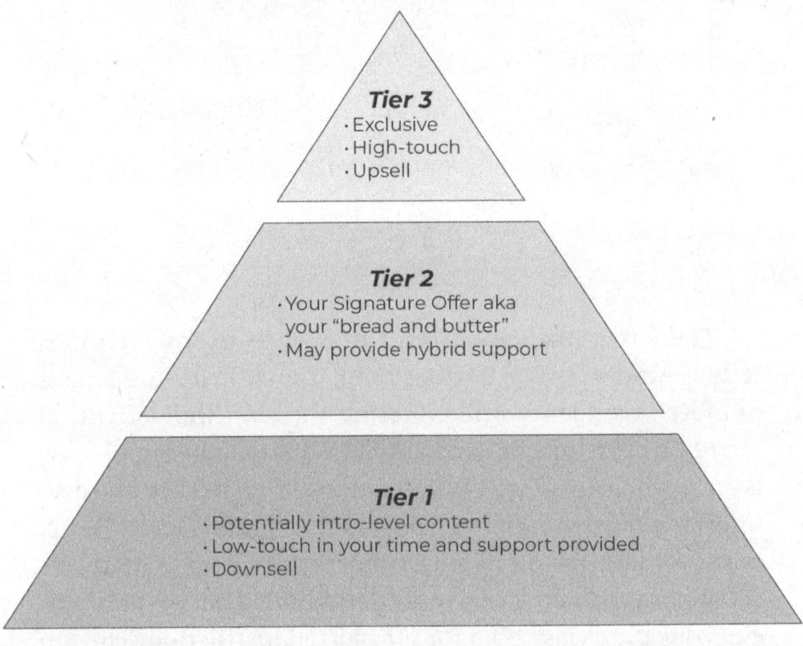

Tier 1 Offer

For our purposes, Tier 1 is potentially introductory-level content. This type of offer is for a client who needs to build foundational knowledge before engaging more deeply with your services. Or if a potential client needs to build more trust with you in order to be more willing to spend more money, a Tier 1 offer could be a downsell, which I'll explain later on in this chapter. Regardless of where the customer is coming from, Tier 1 offers are low touch in terms of how much time and support you're providing. If your business is like your classroom, this is a high-quality intervention that is happening across the entire school. There is very little personalization and customization.

Tier 2 Offer

The next level up is going to be your signature offer. I think of this as your bread and butter. This is the offer you spend the majority of your time marketing, because it's going to be producing the majority of your revenue. But remember, we still aren't personalizing yet. A Tier 2 offer is like pulling a group of students out of the classroom for an extra lesson. This is not high touch (yet). While there's definitely more support than at Tier 1, you have options. The support you offer could be coaching, calls, or a hybrid of asynchronous and synchronous learning. You will perfect your Tier 2 offer over time, because it's the one you will most heavily market and advertise, and the one that will scale.

Tier 3 Offer

Last, your Tier 3 offer is the most intimate, intense, and involved—so it should be exclusive. This offer is extremely high touch, to the point where you likely might not even market it publicly. You may offer Tier 3 only to specific Tier 2 clients that you know are right for it.

Going back to RTI as an analogy, the number of students who receive Tier 3 services is lower than the number of students who receive Tier 2 services, which is lower than the number of students who receive Tier 1 services. The same rules apply to the 7-FigurED Offers framework. The number of clients you're going to have in Tier 3 offer will be fewer than the number in Tier 2 offer and way smaller than the number in Tier 1 offer. Tier 3 is for the smallest, most exclusive number of clients.

Now that you understand the framework, we can bring in examples from education consulting. Let's start with PD, because that's the most common.

Your Tier 1 offer could be a single PD workshop.

Your Tier 2 offer could be a PD series of three to five workshops delivered over a semester.

Your Tier 3 offer could be a comprehensive package for the whole school year that includes a beginning-of-year assessment in September, a customized PD series of workshops, one-on-one coaching with individual teachers, and then an end-of-year assessment in May.

Another example: Let's say instead you are interested in launching a coaching business for first-year math teachers.

Your Tier 1 offer could be a self-paced online course.

Your Tier 2 offer could be a group-coaching program where clients have access to the online course but also have weekly live group-coaching calls with you for 12 weeks.

Your Tier 3 offer could be everything in Tier 1 and Tier 2, PLUS each teacher in the program gets a month of one-on-one coaching sessions with you.

What I want you to notice is that as we move up the pyramid (and into higher tiers), we increase the level of access to you, the amount of support you offer, and also the price. (We'll get to pricing strategies in Chapter 7.) This framework applies to every service model I mentioned earlier in the chapter and, best of all, you can mix and match. For example, let's say you wanted to offer PD, project-based engagements, and speaking engagements. Here's an example of how you could structure those different service models:

Your Tier 1 offer could be a one-time paid speaking engagement.

Your Tier 2 offer could be a short professional development series.

Your Tier 3 offer could be a project-based engagement to create a bespoke training program for new hires based on the concepts from your speaking engagement and PD series.

Consider a "Tier 0"

In addition to Tiers 1 through 3, you may want to develop a "Tier 0" micro-offer that you can deliver quickly, doesn't require a lot of your time, and is almost no-touch in terms of your support. This would be the lowest cost among all your offers. For example, you could have a micro-offer of a 90-minute PD session, a 60-minute one-on-one strategy session, and a single course module. To my clients who are pre-revenue, I recommend they start with a Tier 0 offer, as it builds your confidence while bringing in fast cash. If you choose to do this, you may decide to treat your Tier 1 offer as your signature offer and upsell from there into Tier 2 and Tier 3.

Remember, we're not striving for immediate perfection. Instead, these are starting points. Pick one tier to develop and experiment with. From there, you can build your own unique tiers of offers and evolve your service models as you learn and grow. Trust me, you'll learn through experimentation what works and what doesn't, the service models you like using, and the ones that don't quite fit. The core idea behind tiered offers is that you're giving yourself and your target audience choices at a variety of price points.

The first step is to choose which service models appeal to you, and then think about *possibilities* for offers within those models. Play around with what you could do at Tier 0, Tier 1, Tier 2, Tier 3. Revisit your strengths, your R-E-S, your problem statement. Think about where the most feasible starting place is for you right now to earn some money in the next 30 days.

When you have a rough idea of what your offers and tiers could be, it's time to check your work. Consider how the offers you're building relate to one another. You want to make sure there's a clear path from a small investment (Tier 0 or Tier 1) to a deep partnership (Tier 3). Obviously not every customer is going to take the journey through every tier with you, but many will. If we use the offers for first-year math teachers from earlier on in the chapter, including a Tier 0 micro-offer, you can see how the client relationship and investment deepens as you go along.

Your Tier 0 offer could be one online module.

Your Tier 1 offer could be a self-paced online course.

Your Tier 2 offer could be a group-coaching program where clients have access to the online course and monthly live coaching sessions.

Your Tier 3 offer could be a group coaching program plus one-on-one coaching calls for each client.

Structuring your offers this way allows customers flexibility on price and support while giving you the ability to direct clients to the offer that will create the best results. Let's say an educator presents their Tier 2 offer (group-coaching program) to a potential client who says, "That price is out of my budget." That educator could respond by *down*selling their Tier 1 offer (online course) instead. On the flip side, if the educator pitches their group-coaching program and the potential client says something like, "I want more direct support," then the educator could *up*sell to their Tier 3 offer that includes one-on-one coaching.

There are many reasons and circumstances where it's appropriate to upsell or downsell your offers. The objective is to best serve your potential clients based on their individual needs, because that's what will get the results that builds your business into six figures and beyond. Having a variety of tiered offers at different price points and support levels, with a clear relationship between each of your tiers, easily makes that possible.

CHAPTER 5 REFLECTION QUESTIONS

1. Choose a few service models you'd like to experiment with. Given the problems your business will solve and your unique strengths:

    - What are the pros of this model?

    - What are the cons of this model?

2. Build a menu of potential offers based on your chosen service models. Consider:

    - How do these offers relate?

    - How could your clients shift and grow within these offers?

    - Will these offers make you money right now, or are they the future you'd like your business to grow into?

3. Which of your 7-FigurED Offers set you up to bring revenue into your business in the next 30 days?

ACTION STEPS

- Draft your Tiers 0 through 3.

7-FIGURE EDUCATOR RESOURCES

Visit **www.7febook.com/resources** to:

- Watch Episode 60: "How to Create Irresistible High-Ticket Offers for Your Clients" of the *7-Figure Educator* podcast to learn considerations when building a multiple-five-figure offer

- Watch Episode 33: "Cash Injections: My Strategies to Inject Money Into Your Business Instantly" of the *7-Figure Educator* podcast to dive deeper into Tier 0 offers

Claim Your Client

Objective: Define who you want to work with

I remember vividly one afternoon as a principal when a student asked to meet with me. In that meeting, they bravely shared that they identified as transgender and that bathroom breaks during class had become some of the most uncomfortable moments of their day. This was my first experience supporting a transgender student, and I quickly realized this was not a moment for quick fixes or ready-made solutions. This was a moment that required me to sit, be present, and listen deeply. We talked for nearly 40 minutes that day, and we ate lunch together the next day to continue the conversation.

Through those conversations, I began to understand their reality in a way I could not have grasped otherwise. Together, we were able to create a path forward, an experience that honored their identity while also navigating district policies that were not designed with their needs in mind. That is the power of listening: It transforms leadership into partnership, shifts power dynamics, and creates the conditions for change. Listening is not simply about hearing words; it is about honoring our shared humanity.

Listening is not a passive act. It is a powerful tool for justice. One of the hallmarks of white supremacy is paternalism: the idea that decisions should be made for people without their input. That absence of listening has caused generations of harm in schools, communities, and systems. To truly listen is to disrupt that cycle. It means decentering yourself long enough to honor the lived experience of someone else. Listening requires humility, openness, and the courage to hold space for perspectives that may challenge your own.

In business, the same principle applies. Claiming your client begins not with flashy marketing tactics or assumptions about what people need, but with listening. Just as I had to quiet my own perspective to truly understand my student's experience, you must listen deeply to your clients to understand theirs. Market research is not about collecting data points to fit into a neat profile—it is about honoring the voices of the people you are called to serve. When you listen with intention, you uncover not just demographics, but desires, frustrations, and aspirations. It is what allows you to build a client avatar that isn't based on stereotypes or assumptions, but on truth. Listening is the starting point for justice in leadership, and it is also the foundation for building a business that makes real impact.

Spending money is an act of trust. To your target client you are a stranger, and you have to earn the right to make an offer. Your ideal client exists, and they are ready to invest in your services, but in order to attract those people, you have to be really, really clear in your messaging. You have to be consistent in your visibility and how you show up. You have to get in the weeds and *really* know what they're about. You earn the trust of your target audience by knowing them like you know your best friend.

I have known my best friend, Ashley, since college. We're similar in some ways and very different in others, but because we've been close for 20 years, I can complete her sentences. I know that the quickest way to make her upset is to treat others disrespectfully. I know what's gonna get her feelin' some kinda way. I know what's gonna make her happy. I know what types of gifts that she wants. I know how she'll want to spend her birthday. I can predict the choices she's going to make, because I know how she thinks. I know her like I know myself.

And that's how you are going to know your client by the end of this chapter.

You might be thinking, *But Erica, I already know my client, because she's a principal and I was a principal.*

Or *I know exactly what my clients want, because I used to teach their kids.*

Respectfully? You don't know. Yet.

Becoming best friends with your target client is what we're going to focus on in this chapter. I'm going to share my unique approach to identifying your target client and show you how to build a target-client profile based on what you know today. I'll describe two common mistakes that educators make in this process and show you how to test your profile with real-life people. By the end of this chapter, you will know your client as well as your bestie to be able to craft a marketing message that speaks to them directly.

LISTENING TO LEARN

Before we dig into the how, it's important to understand why deep listening is the best way to approach the work you're about to do. This is especially applicable for educators, because we've had to operate within a system that does not listen to folks, especially folks who have been historically marginalized. Because if the system *did* listen to people, then it would actually create solutions in everyone's best interest, and all the data—around student learning, teacher retention, standardized testing, graduation rates—would be much better than what we have today.

As educators who know a lot about our target audience in the classroom, it can be easy to underestimate listening, to write it off, to assume that you already know what you need to know. Or that you're already listening, because you're physically present in a conversation. But it's possible to send a survey, have a coffee chat over Zoom, and ask important questions without truly listening in a way that will make a difference to your business.

Active listening is actually a complex strategy that has been shown to sharpen our ability to detect other people's emotions, understand our own, and use all that information to guide interactions (and in business, make sales). As business owners, we can use listening as a strategy to collect data about our target client that can shape our marketing messages and the services we offer. Later on in this chapter, I'm going to ask you to conduct informational interviews with your target clients as a way to do market research. In those interviews, and in fact from now on, I want you to take the approach of a data scientist looking for facts and stories and narratives with an open, observational mind.

I completed a listening orientation with educator, leadership coach, facilitator, and author of *The Listening Leader* Shane Safir. Safir's framework of the Listening Leader demonstrates how careful and intentional listening can generate positive change for all by allowing you to tune in to the dominant narrative, keep a finger on the pulse of change, stay true to personal values, and model compassion (among other benefits). This model is valuable inside of schools and education more broadly, but also holds important lessons for educators like you and me who want to translate our skills to business.

Listening Leaders share six key characteristics:

- Leaders bring people together from a bold vision.

- Leaders see relationships as key to results.

- Leaders view listening as a way to gather data.

- Leaders hold a long-term perspective (i.e., are "in it for the long haul").

- Leaders gather input but then take action.

- Leaders are viewed as trustworthy, visionary, and high integrity.

To demonstrate how to start showing up in this way, Safir outlines three strategic listening stances educators can take in conversations with stakeholders. Used in your business, these stances can help frame questions that will allow you to collect data while also providing insight to your target audience.

Strategic Listening Stance #1: Orientation to Vision

Look for opportunities to connect what your target audience cares about with your vision for your business and its impact. For example, my desired outcome is to make every educator I meet a millionaire. In conversations with my target audience, I'm going to ask questions with that outcome in mind while keeping an open stance of listening. Potential roadblocks for my target audience could include finances, or mindset, or skills, or knowledge. Or their challenge could be something I don't know about yet. I don't have an opinion about what's in their way. Instead, I'm listening with curiosity and the simple intention of learning about my target audience's experiences. By doing so, I learn more about my target audience and how to create offers that both align to my vision and help them.

Strategic Listening Stance #2: Reflective Inquiry

It's important to ask thought-provoking questions that allow your target audience to expand their thinking and perspective on the problem that your business solves. Asking open-ended questions like, "What are your hopes and fears about . . ." and "What could be getting in your way of . . .?" allows you to tap into the emotions and challenges your target audience is experiencing. Understanding those visceral feelings is part of creating marketing messages that resonate. If you follow me on Instagram, you'll see me doing this all the time. I ask questions like, "What happens if you just say no?" and "Do you actually want it, or were you told to want it?" because that gets my client thinking and allows me to respond to their concerns and emotions in ways that resonate.

Strategic Listening Stance #3: Bias to Action

In her book, Safir states that leaders can tap into "the need for autonomy and agency with questions that prompt thoughtful action." In other words, asking the right questions can invite people to think about, play with, and, crucially, *act* on new ideas. What this could sound like in a conversation with your target audience might be something like, "What are one or two things that you could take action on?"

You as the business owner should be biased to act as well. So often, I'm asked things like, "Should I package this in a membership?" or "Should I do a full day of PD, or offer only a half day?" and my answer is always that I don't know. Because I'm not your target audience. You as the listening leader can be biased to action by asking your target audience what makes the most sense *for them*. And once they tell you, run the play.

Over the years, I've found that listening is more effective than reading any statistic or survey. While I was writing this chapter, I was getting ready to launch a new program. While preparing, I made sure to give my audience a preview and ask for feedback—because I want to hear what y'all think. That was true when I was a four-figure entrepreneur, and it's still gonna be true when my business grows to eight figures and beyond. Listening is that critical to my success and to yours.

Having a listening orientation in your business allows you to collect data that's outside of what you can gather from the formal methodology we often defer to in education. After all, data isn't limited to white papers, standardized tests and scores, and rubrics and surveys. While the status quo of white-supremacy culture demands "worship of the written word," as business owners we can choose to believe in the lived experiences of our target audience. After all, I don't need a working paper to show me why Black educators are leaving the classroom at higher rates than white ones when I've got teachers telling me their stories in my DMs.

By making the time and effort to listen, I know what's up with my target audience, and so will you. So, while you read this chapter and consider who your target client is, think about how careful and truly intentional listening would impact how your business could help that person. How could you look beyond what you think you know to be true and really listen to others? What is the path and the power of listening in your business? Because, as Safir says, leaders recognize that the data we need is right before us if we choose to listen.

DEFINING YOUR TARGET CLIENTS

Your target client has trust issues.

I can say that with confidence, because nearly *everyone* has trust issues when it comes to spending money. Between the revolving door of leaders in education, the constant changes in government regulations, the subpar consultants out there delivering crap PD, and the constant barrage of advertising we're all subjected to in every aspect of our lives, your target client has reason to be skeptical.

But they're still ready and going to spend money if and when you put in the work to get their attention, listen to their experience, gain their trust, and show how you can help. That's true regardless of who you want to work with or at whatever price point you want to charge. The person you want to help and who is willing to pay you to get that help exists. There are often thousands, sometimes millions, of them. But sometimes our own mindset can get in the way of that reality. The minute you think about their bank account—and not the value of what you can offer—you begin to hedge.

Instead, let me offer an important reframe. Your client wants to trust, they want to change, and they want to work with you and will be happy to pay for your services at whatever price point . . . when you show that you understand their experience. When you listen and learn their pain points. When you are consistent in where, when, and how you show up. (More on that in Chapter 9.) The confidence with which you speak and the words you use matter. The depth of your knowledge about your client matters. These folks aren't just your target clients—instead, I call them TCFs (Target Client Friend) because you need to know them as well as you would know a friend.

Because let's be real, it's not enough to simply know demographic information. Going back to my own bestie as an example, to know Ashley, it would not be enough to know that she is a 39-year-old Black woman who lives in Columbus, Ohio, and works as an attorney. Those are basic facts, sure, but those details could belong to any number of people. That's not *Ashley*. If I had to describe my best friend, I might say that she's deeply empathetic. She leads with the spirit of curiosity. When she is in conversation one-on-one with you, she will make you feel like the only person in a crowded room, because she will be lost in discovering more about you. She is happier at home trying a new recipe and catching up with a friend than she is hitting the town on a Saturday night. Those details show that I have beyond a surface-level understanding of her, right?

That level of intimacy and detail is where you get to truly know your clients. We build trust by showing respect for our TCF's desires and deeply understanding their needs. Working from a TCF mindset allows us to lead with curiosity and form better relationships from the jump. That's why I created and continue to use the acronym *TCF* instead of a more transactional term like *ideal client*.

Let's start by taking a moment to visualize your own best friend. How would you describe that person to someone else? You likely wouldn't cite the demographic details, just like I wouldn't describe Ashley as a 39-year-old Black woman from Columbus, Ohio. Instead you would get personal. For example, I might mention that she works in estate planning because she is an empath who cares deeply about supporting Black families to build generational wealth. In that description, you get who Ashley is and maybe how she would show up in certain situations and circumstances. There's a deep level of understanding and intimacy.

That's the orientation you're aiming for with your own TCF. The better understanding you have of your target client, the tighter and clearer your marketing message will be. The more intimately you know their dreams and goals, the more you will be able to speak to the value and transformation you will provide. The more you resonate with and reflect their feelings and emotions, the more TCFs you will attract and convert into paying clients. And that will directly relate to the amount of money you bring into your business.

CREATING YOUR TCF PROFILE

Now that you understand the perspective and depth we're bringing to this work, let's get into the step-by-step. Even though demographics alone are not good enough, we do need to understand those facts to start. I encourage you to drill down. You can certainly include basics like gender, racial background, ethnicity, and location. But you could also consider years of experience, whether your TCF works in a rural area, suburbia, or in urban settings. Does your TCF work in Title I schools? Or are they working in suburban, affluent schools? Private or maybe even tribal schools?

A common demographic data point is occupation. For some of you, that's going to be easy and clear, because you work with teachers or you work with principals. But the question of occupation could be more nuanced. For instance, I know educators who work with teacher leaders. How might you define that? What is a teacher leader's title? In some districts the role would be called a dean; in other places it is called a facilitator or instructional coach. What might differentiate the titles or job descriptions of your TCF? Be as holistic about these details as possible.

From there, consider how your TCF is experiencing the problem that your business solves. When you're brainstorming this aspect of your TCF profile, consider their day-to-day experiences. What frustrations are your TCFs having? How about the obstacles—perceived or real—between them and their desired outcomes? What's preventing them from coming up with or implementing a solution to their problem on their own? What are the pain points that you can help resolve? You wanna be as specific as possible here of how the problem is showing up in their everyday lives.

Go beyond the surface. This is where you literally need to describe their experience—like it's a movie trailer where your TCF is the main character and you're watching the problem play out scene by scene. Get to that level of specificity of how they're experiencing the problem. When you really dig down, what's the biggest hurdle to finding a solution? Is it access? How about time? Overwhelm? Feeling stuck about how to start? Are they consumed with what others will think? Go deep.

To show you how this is done, I'm going to share an example of a TCF profile from my Get LaunchED Consulting program that this book is based on. (And, fair warning, get ready to recognize yourself.)

> Megan is an eighth-year ELA teacher in New York City. Each year she is one of the highest-performing teachers in her school and district. She absolutely loves her content and takes advantage of every opportunity to attend professional development. She has a master's in reading intervention from Teachers College at Columbia University and is a district trainer for literacy. Through delivering PD for her district, she has realized how much she loves teaching other adults. She also learned how most teachers don't have access to training on effective reading practices. She wants to start an education consulting business training teachers in these practices but has no idea where to start. She's wondering how she can start a business while still working full-time.

You'll notice there are a few key questions answered in the TCF profile of Megan.

What are the demographics of our TCF? Current occupation?

Megan is an eighth-year ELA teacher in New York City. . . . She has a master's in reading intervention from Teachers College . . . and is a district trainer for literacy.

How are they experiencing your problem?

She also learned how most teachers don't have access to training on effective reading practices.

What have been some of their biggest hurdles in finding a solution?

She wants to start an education consulting business training teachers in [effective reading] practices but has no idea where to start. She's wondering how she can start a business while still working full-time.

But we can go further. Let's talk about what's not in these answers but is equally important for a Get LaunchED Consulting TCF. In terms of demographic information, you'll notice Megan is not a new teacher. That's intentional, because my TCFs are educators who have more than five years of experience. Similarly, I work with people who are already excellent at what they do. Megan checks that box because she has an advanced degree and has been elevated to a trainer for her district. She has a very clear level of expertise in ELA instruction and reading instruction.

Next, we can dig into how Megan is experiencing the problem. In this profile, I say that she has learned that most teachers don't have access to training on effective reading practices. That's an interesting kind of data point because it assumes that she has gathered this information from working with teachers and realizing some of them don't have the access or knowledge she does. Which means there's a business opportunity for her. From her profile, we know she's realized that there's an opportunity, but she's stuck on how to start while still at her full-time teaching job. This is valuable information for me, because I can be mindful of the fact that my services need to accommodate people who are working a full-time job.

You can see how every detail I put into the TCF profile matters and gives me data points that inform my business. Because I know all these things about Megan, I can start to brainstorm how I might meet and interact with more clients like her, both online and in person. Are there alumni groups Megan would belong to? What Facebook groups would she join? What conferences would she attend? Similarly, I can start to structure my services to better work for clients like her. Because I know that she is just getting started, I know my offers need to include foundational content. I know my delivery has to be manageable for someone working full-time in a school. By knowing my TCF intimately and clearly, I can start to conceive and execute strategies to meet and build relationships that eventually lead to sales, contracts, and revenue.

Now that you understand both what a TCF profile looks like and what its purpose can be, I can help you avoid common mistakes I've seen my clients make in this step of their business.

TCF Mistake #1: Assuming that your experience is their experience

If you want to serve math teachers, 9.9 times out of 10, you've been a math teacher.

If you want to serve principals, 9.9 times out of 10, you've been a principal.

Is this a big assumption I'm making, given that we've probably never met?

Definitely, and yet I'm probably right. There's nothing wrong with serving folks where you used to be and where you have the most experience in both the problem and the solution. However, where the missteps creep up is when you rely too heavily on your own experience to inform your TCF profile. When we're familiar with who we serve, it can be tempting to believe that we already know what their struggles are like and what problems they need solved. But the truth is that you don't know everything you need to know about your target client solely from your own experience.

Partly that's because you know too much. You are an expert, and when you're an expert, it's often tricky to speak the language of a novice. To draw an analogy from sports, the expert version of you is like Michael Jordan at the top of his game, and your TCF may be more like the 15-year-old who got cut from his high school varsity team. You need to understand both perspectives to create an effective TCF profile.

In short, just because you've been your target client doesn't mean that you know everything there is to know about them. Instead, apply Safir's Listening Leader principles from earlier in the chapter and remove yourself and your experience from the TCF profile (at least at first) and put your focus on deep listening. Allow yourself to adopt a mindset of curiosity and let your TCF tell you what's going on with them. This approach allows you to get close to their experience and capture the language they use to describe it, which you can use in both your profile and your future marketing. While your own experience can *inform* what you end up creating, you're letting your target clients lead even when creating your own internal strategy.

This is especially important in fields and focus areas where educators adopt and use a lot of jargon, like diversity, equity and inclusion (DEI) work, for example. While it may be common for facilitators and experts to use words like *co-conspirator* or *ally*, when you are considering your marketing message, you have to consider whether your target client uses those words. If they don't, then you shouldn't be using that language in your marketing either, even if every one of your competitors does. Use the language that your target client uses. Being able to step into their experience—whether it mirrors yours or not—is key to understanding the problem your business solves from their perspective.

TCF Mistake #2: Not understanding who your true client is

Every business has a stakeholder that signs your contract. That may be an individual person that you serve and help directly—for example, a teacher, a parent, a counselor, or a principal. But your stakeholder could be different from the person you directly work with. Going back to our example of DEI work, let's say that your business helps school districts implement a hiring initiative supporting candidates from diverse backgrounds. Even if you would be eventually working with individual principals on this initiative, your actual TCF would be the decision-makers within the district who can green-light the kind of district-wide programming you offer. That's a subtle but important difference.

To understand who your TCF really is, you need to understand your overarching business model. There are two: what are known as B2B (business to business) and B2C (business-to-consumer). In a B2B model, your contract is going to be with another business—a school, a district, a nonprofit, maybe an educational organization or parent-teacher association. Note that you may still be serving individual educators or even individuals outside of education (like parents), but your *contract* is with another business or organization. In contrast, when you have a B2C model, your contract or client agreement is with an individual. Maybe you have a tutoring company where you contract with parents to work with students. That's B2C. Or maybe you coach individual teachers in both one-on-one and group settings. That would be B2C if the teachers were paying you themselves. If you were doing the same coaching but instead the district was paying you, that would be B2B.

Within education, this can get sticky, because you can have a situation where a client uses PD funds from their job to pay you, but the contract is in their name. That's still a B2C model even though they're using PD funds from their employer. What differentiates B2B from B2C is who signs the contract, not necessarily who pays.

Though it can be tempting to use both models, you need to choose one for your business. In addition to helping you create an effective TCF profile, choosing a model to operate with is going to allow you to stay focused and make quick decisions in future chapters.

TESTING YOUR TCF

Now that you know how to create a TCF profile and what common missteps to avoid, we can talk about "testing" your work. After creating a rough draft of your TCF profile, you're going to schedule and hold three to five 30-minute informational interviews with people that you think fit the description of your TCF. The goal is to ask at least three questions that will help you better understand your client's perspective on the problem that your business solves and test their interest in the offers you outlined in Chapter 5.

You can use e-mail, text, or social media to reach out to your network to help you gather folks for these informational interviews. While you can interview people you already know, this can also be a great way to practice being visible and making an ask from your broader community (online or in person). A great strategy is to post or send a story or testimony from your own experience and a teaser of the result your business means to provide, because that helps people understand why you're asking. Within that post or e-mail or text, be sure to include a time-bound call to action so your request has urgency and no one's tempted to let your ask linger.

Here are a couple examples of these asks so you understand exactly what to say. Remember my TCF Megan from earlier in the chapter? My market research for that TCF profile began with a series of Instagram stories I posted back in 2020 where I made my ask. The story was a photo of me with this text (being added line by line so folks could read along):

Three years ago, I took a leap of faith and started my own consulting business. It allowed me to do work that I love, developing school leaders. Eight months later, I paid off all of my credit card debt. I built my savings to resign from my job and move 13 hours away to start a full-time doctoral program.

This is what I mean by testimony. I'm sharing details from my R-E-S statement to share what I've done so far. The post went on:

I believe you can lead from your values and have a social impact without sacrificing financial freedom. I'm working to build a small program to help other educators launch their own education consulting business. As an educator, I'm a stickler for meaningful learning experiences. So, I'm gathering info to help me build a transformative program.

Here, I'm giving a teaser of what I'm building. Note that I don't need all the details yet, because that's what these informational interviews will help to inform.

If you're an educator who has considered starting a consulting business, but not sure where to start, I wanna talk to you. DM me if that's you. I'm looking to connect for 30 minutes with about three to five people by the end of the week.

I'm concluding with who I'm specifically looking for (broad demographics are fine) and making a clear, time-bound request to meet. From these posts I was able to interview five people.

Here's another example from my client Jessica, who shared her ask on Facebook. Her post said:

Two years ago, I took on a side gig teaching English and science virtually to pay my grad school tuition. Virtual education has grown into a passion of mine as a vehicle for quality education. But in today's times, virtual education came quickly and without time to prepare. It left many amazing teachers feeling overwhelmed and inadequate.

That is not okay.

For Jessica, the beginning of this post combines her R-E-S and problem statement. The next sentence talks about what she's creating.

I'm working to create a fast, accessible, and effective course for teachers to learn to teach virtually.

And then she makes a clear, time-bound request that includes who she wants to talk to:

But I need to know what you need, teachers. If you are willing to talk about your strengths, areas for growth, and concerns for virtual education, please DM me.

Jessica received over 90 reactions, 11 comments, and 21 shares from her network, which made it easy to book the informational interviews she was looking for. Like Jessica, you may be pleasantly surprised by how people show up and support you when you let folks know what you're doing and especially *why*.

Remember, the purpose of this post and the TCF interviews aren't to sell anyone on your services. Instead, this is market research. That said, if someone does ask about your services on the call, you can simply say that you'll be rolling out services soon and that you'd be happy to add their e-mail to your e-mail list so they will be the first to know when you launch.

You can share your testimony and request to talk through text, e-mail, on social media, or a combination of all three. It pays to be thoughtful in *how* you make the ask, both in terms of what you say and the medium you use. While it can feel safer to tap your existing network of friends and colleagues to conduct these informational interviews, there is a lot of value added when you make your ask on social media. Posting on social media automatically starts to build general awareness around your work. Similarly, social media can plant a seed, create interactions, and begin to build relationships with people outside of your current network who could be potential clients or referral partners in the future.

If you have a small following on social media that's mostly friends and family, or haven't been on social media consistently, fewer people will see and respond to your post, lessening its impact. That's when it's smart to use all your resources, including leveraging e-mail and text to ask folks you already know—or go old-school and ask your direct network to share with *their* networks too.

When you're ready to make your ask, take the time to sketch out three to five interview questions. Consider what you don't know about your TCF. When I did my informational interviews for Get LaunchED Consulting, I asked questions like:

"Why are you interested in education consulting?"

"What are the two to three biggest questions you have related to education consulting?" "Have you participated in small-group coaching before? What was powerful about that experience? What (if anything) would you change?"

Be sure to record these informational interviews (with permission, of course) and use an AI tool to transcribe the call so that you can use the interviewees' exact language in both your TCF profile and in future marketing. (This is gold, y'all.)

Remember that the goal of these TCF interviews is to help you design offers and an overall client experience that will resonate with exactly who you want to work with.

How to ask about pricing

Instead of "how much would you pay for . . .," come into your informational interviews with a range in mind. (And read ahead to Chapter 7 if you have zero idea what your range should be.) When I did market research for Get LaunchED Consulting, I asked if people would pay $2,000 to $5,000 for a small group-coaching program that helped them start their education consulting business. Then I asked if the range felt too high, too low, or just right. Mind you, I wasn't basing my prices on any one person's budget but rather the general sense I was able to gauge off my own research. Then I was able to use the responses from my informational interviews to refine my range.

CHAPTER 6 REFLECTION QUESTIONS

1. How can you incorporate Listening Leader principles throughout your business?

2. Which of the two TCF mistakes resonates with you the most, and what steps do you need to take to avoid making that mistake in your business?

3. How will having a TCF profile influence your business?

ACTION STEPS

- Draft a preliminary sketch of your Target Client Friend based on what you already know.

  - What are their demographics?

  - What is their current occupation?

  - How are they experiencing your problem?

  - What are their pain points?

  - What have been some of their biggest hurdles in finding a solution?

  - Is your TCF another business (i.e., B2B) or a consumer (B2C)?

- Consider: What data are you missing from your preliminary TCF profile? (Hint: This is what you want to find out in your informational interviews.)

- Script the communication you will use to recruit 3 to 5 informational interviews.

  - Name the problem.

  - Name a piece of your R-E-S.

  - Include a teaser of what you're planning to create (service model, outcome, etc.).

  - Include a time-bound call to action.

- Script interview questions for your TCFs that allow you to better understand their pain points and improve upon the rough draft TCF profile.

- Conduct 3 to 5 informational interviews with your TCFs.

- Revise your TCF profile by incorporating the information you've gathered in the interviews (and update your problem statement if needed).

7-FIGURE EDUCATOR RESOURCES

Visit **www.7febook.com/resources** to:

- Review examples of social media communication to request informational interviews

- Grab a copy of *The Listening Leader* by Shane Safir

- Watch Episode 73: "From NASA to CEO: A 7-FigurED™ Hot Seat w/ Dr. Teneka Steed" of the *7-Figure Educator* podcast, a live hot-seat episode where I coach a member of our community in redefining their TCF

Pick Your Pricing

Objective: Set your pricing for your tiered offers

When Alicia spotted me across the room at a recent pop-up in Atlanta, she practically sprinted over. Her smile was wide, but her voice told a different story. She blurted out, "Dr. EJT, I did it! I booked my biggest deal yet." Then, before I could even congratulate her, her shoulders sank. "But . . . I undercharged."

She went on to explain: "At the time, $35,000 felt like a dream number. I sold a professional development package to a middle school that included two full-day site visits each month. On top of that, every single member of the leadership team gets one-on-one coaching. I even offered to do the coaching during their planning periods so it wouldn't disrupt their day." She let out a deep sigh. "But here's the thing . . . all of that coaching and PD had to happen on-site. Which means the travel costs are through the roof! Traveling alone is eating into my profit. I never built those costs into the proposal."

Alicia had made a rookie mistake when it comes to pricing. She hadn't factored in how much time would be required to deliver on what she had promised and hadn't considered all the expenses. For this particular contract, Alicia showing up to the school two times per month wasn't actually that big of a deal. But the one-on-one coaching was a different story. There were eight people on the leadership team, each of whom needed their own time with Alicia—also in person, also at the school, and typically not on the same day or even at the same time of day.

So, instead of 2 days per month, Alicia ended up spending up to 10 days every month at a single school. That meant half of her time to deliver services was being gobbled up by just one contract. Because the scheduling was inconsistent, she couldn't even fill the gaps with hourly work. Worst of all, because the school was an hour away thanks to traffic, Alicia needed to fill her car up with gas at least twice a week. When she'd submitted the proposal, $35,000 had sounded like a win, but within a month of starting the contract, Alicia was frustrated. The travel costs, the long days on-site, and the hours of one-on-one coaching quickly added up, and she realized the contract was demanding far more time and money than she'd planned. What felt like a breakthrough deal was instead re-creating the same cycle of being overworked and underpaid that she thought she had left behind in her 9-to-5.

Alicia learned a powerful lesson that every entrepreneur is faced with. Always, always, *always* run your numbers. And after you run them once, run them again.

Let me be real: Pricing is complex. Mistakes like Alicia's are common when folks are first starting out. Partly that's because there is no standard formula, approach, or even a set range that consultants need to follow in education—or in any industry, really. The upside of "no rules" is that as entrepreneurs, pricing is yet another area where we get to create our own. But where there are no rules, that can often be where oppression lives. The ugly truth of "no rules" is that if you have not worked on your money mindset and begun the work to heal your relationship with money, you will perpetuate the cycle of being undervalued.

In this chapter, I'm going to teach you how to run your numbers and use your own data to figure out how to price each of your offers. We'll start with an explanation of how pricing relates to wealth creation so you get a seven-figure view of how pricing will evolve as you and your business grow together. With that context, I'll share the biggest mindset hurdles I see in my clients so you don't get caught up, and then I'll explain two different broad approaches to pricing: market based and value based. We'll revisit the tiers of offers you outlined in Chapter 5 as well as look at pricing guidelines for your business model (B2B or B2C). Last, we'll talk about how to use your expenses and desired take-home salary to set prices and "check" that you'll meet the financial goals you have for yourself and your business.

By the end of this chapter, you will know how to set, and more importantly *adjust*, your prices in a way that attracts your Target Client Friends, gets them to convert into paying clients, and moves you closer to your Freedom and Abundance Numbers.

BEFORE WE BEGIN

Throughout this chapter, I'm going to refer to pricing as a journey. What I mean by that is that your prices are going to change as you and your business do. In Chapter 5, I told you that one of the most common mistakes that new entrepreneurs make is not having scalable offers. There's a similar issue in pricing, which is not understanding how your businesses and overall careers generate wealth.

Since 2013, founder Nathan Barry has grown his e-mail marketing software, Kit, from $0 to nearly $50 million in annual revenue. In 2019, he wrote a blog about the ladders of wealth creation for entrepreneurs. Everyone, he said, starts out on the first ladder, exchanging time for money at someone else's company. In short: You have a job. You step on the second ladder to wealth when you start a business. As discussed in Chapter 6, it can be smart to charge an hourly rate when you're just starting your business. You're still determining the time and expenses involved in delivering your services. However, the idea is to charge by the hour only long enough to figure out what you should charge by the project or in a flat fee.

The third step to wealth creation is when your business sells packages of services, and/or has a team delivering services directly to clients. This is when you set prices based on the value you create rather than the time and expenses involved in delivery. I'll show you how to do this later on in this chapter.

What I want you to recognize is that as you move up the ladder, your pricing becomes scalable right alongside your offers and your team. It's important to take the full journey of pricing and work your way up the ladder, because each step to creating wealth has its own unique and rich lessons to learn. You have to start out charging hourly so that you understand all the money involved from your expenses to the value you deliver. Then you have to sort out what would be profitable for individual projects so that eventually you can sell packages or hire a team to help you deliver. The objective is to learn as you grow.

The same can be said for your money mindset. If you aren't clear on your money mindset when you start setting your pricing, you will self-sabotage, either consciously or unconsciously. Getting your mind right before determining how to price your services is important. There are three common beliefs that I see in my clients and that I've held myself when it comes to pricing. If these are present for you, that's not a good or bad thing. In fact, I would argue that you're pretty darn normal. But I want you to be aware of how mindset issues crop up so that you can recognize when you're getting in your own way—and shift that.

1. Doubting, either consciously or unconsciously, that people will pay for your services

This belief will cause you to undercharge and to also feel uncomfortable when you realize you need to raise your prices to cover costs and generate profit. If this isn't you: cool. But if this resonates even a little bit, I want you to revisit your R-E-S and remind yourself of who you are. Not everybody can do what you do. Not everybody has accomplished what you have accomplished. You are unique. And because you've got those receipts, those experiences, those skills, people will be willing to pay you for the solutions that only you can deliver.

Later on in this chapter, I'm going to explain an approach that uses what your competitors charge as a benchmark for your own pricing. By using this market-based approach, you'll be able to understand what others are receiving in exchange for the value they provide (which may be similar, but not as good as what you'll deliver).

2. Assuming clients won't be able to afford what you want to charge

I've heard this over and over and over again from fellow entrepreneurs both inside and outside education. But the truth I want to anchor you in is that your client's bank account is none of your business. You don't know what's in so-and-so's budget, ever . . . until they tell you. If you haven't asked and they haven't answered, you don't know. Making assumptions about your client's bank account sounds like "schools don't have a lot of money" or "a small organization like that won't be able to afford it." Take a moment and visualize the first three letters of assumption—aka what we make of ourselves when we make assumptions about our clients' budgets. Especially when you start offering discounts or knocking down the price before you even ask what their budget actually is.

The truth is that people afford what they value. Some people will spend hundreds or even thousands to buy a brand-new cowboy outfit and tickets to see Beyoncé on tour, because that's what that experience is worth to them. The clients who are not a fit for you may say they can't afford it, because they aren't able to see the value (yet) of what you bring to the table. In contrast, the clients who are a great fit will always see your value and will pay accordingly. Shifting your mindset from "no one will pay" to "the right people will pay" is small but significant.

3. Believing that you have to set prices once and stick with that forever

When I first started, I charged $1,600 for a day of PD.

As I'm writing this in the summer of 2025, I charge $25,000 for a day of PD. And by the time this book comes out, my price will likely have increased again.

I share this to show that you can grow into pricing and change what you charge over time as you start to feel more confident and clear about the results you can deliver. I want you to give yourself the permission to see the prices you're about to set as a starting point, knowing you have the right to change your mind. So if a number like $10,000 feels really uncomfortable, you can decide to start at $5,000. After a few contracts, you might increase your fee to $7,000 or $8,000. The point is that you get to choose a price that feels good to you.

The first person who has to believe in your pricing is you

Throughout this chapter, I'm going to share ranges of pricing for each of the tiers and business models you learned about in Chapter 5. If, while reading this chapter, you feel your body temperature begin to rise, start to feel tense or anxious, or simply notice that your thoughts are saying *I can't*—take a breath.

Pricing is a journey. When you're unsure about your pricing, your clients can smell it a mile away. Remember that you can choose a lower starting point for your pricing that you can say with your chest and confidently communicate to your client. As you continue to deliver your services and witness the transformation you create for your clients, your confidence in your pricing will increase over time. The objective of the work you do in this chapter isn't to set the highest price you can or will ever for your services. Instead, it's to set pricing that you feel confident about and that makes your business profitable.

MARKET-BASED PRICING

This first approach to pricing is based on the economic principle of supply and demand. This approach prioritizes affordability and access in order to maximize the number of people who buy. I want to be really clear that using market-based pricing doesn't mean that your services are low quality. You still have to provide quality results for clients. However, with this approach, you intentionally keep your expenses and prices low and reduce your profit margin per service to make sure your offers are accessible. This more budget-friendly price point positions you to sell a higher *volume* of services.

An example of market-based pricing in the real world is the evolution in pricing of flat-screen TVs. I don't know if y'all remember back in the day when flat-screen TVs were new, but back then, they were valued as a luxury good. Folks would be lined up outside of RadioShack on Black Friday, ready to tussle for their brand new flat-screen. You had to drop at least a thousand dollars, maybe even two, to get one in your house. But today you can buy a quality flat-screen TV for a few hundred dollars. The companies producing these TVs are no longer looking to be exclusive. They now charge a price point that is accessible to most, because they are looking for sales volume and mass-market appeal.

Now let's look at an education consulting example. A few years ago, I saw a consultant offering a virtual workshop for $200, with a 20 percent discount for groups of four or more. At the time, this educator had over 800 people enrolled.

Grabs calculator

The educator earned over $160,000 from that workshop alone, using accessible, market-based pricing. I'm sharing this example specifically because market-based pricing doesn't have to mean bargain-basement pricing.

The key to market-based pricing is volume. Because you're at a lower price point, in order to bring in significant revenue, you've gotta have numbers. Consider the workshop I just mentioned. Given that the price was $200, to make a good profit, that educator needed more than 10 to 15 people registered. By making the price point relatively affordable, they were looking to attract hundreds or maybe even thousands of customers. Here's another example, this time from my own business. I have some one-off modules that are repackaged replays from workshops that I've done. I sell these for $50 to $200 online, because I'm not trying to be exclusive with these particular offers. These are available to everyone at an accessible price point. However, remember that because you are prioritizing affordability and access, you must also prioritize volume. Because you need a high number of clients, you must reach a lot of people at once. To make this approach to pricing work, you have to first grow a large audience that is aware of your brand before you make any kind of pitch. You can't expect to run the market-based pricing play if you're launching to 300 Instagram followers, where only 30 of those people will see your posts and only 3 will buy.

With this approach you also want to prioritize breadth over depth. Because this is a lower-price-point offer, you're not going super deep. Market-based pricing best applies to Tier 1 services. (If you have decided to include a "Tier 0" or micro-offer, then everything I'm about to say regarding Tier 1 applies to your Tier 0 offer as well.) As a reminder from Chapter 5, Tier 1 is your entry-level content. These offers are low touch in terms of your time and the support you provide. Again, this could be something like a live workshop, a repackaged video of a workshop you've already held, or a digital product. These types of offers allow for high sales volume, which is why Tier 1 is the perfect place to experiment with market-based pricing.

To be 100 percent clear, let's go through some examples:

If you decide to do a live workshop for $97, that's a Tier 1 offer. If you decide to do a live workshop for $97 and then repackage the replay for $47, that's still a Tier 1 offer. If you decide to sell a self-paced online course where there is no live coaching or support outside of what's already been pre-recorded for $2,500, that's still a Tier 1 offer. Market-based pricing typically always applies to Tier 1 offers even if your "lowest" price is thousands of dollars.

This may go without saying, but when you do market-based pricing, you gotta know the market. That's how you determine what the price should be. There are a few strategies for figuring out what your market wants. The first should be obvious: Survey your TCFs. You can even include questions in your informational interviews like:

"In the past, how much have you paid for [offer]?"

"When you have attended [offer], how much did it cost?"

"I'm thinking of charging $X for my [offer]—do you think that's too high, too low, or just right?"

If asking directly feels awkward, you can create an online survey that you share with TCFs you've already interviewed or online with your followers or network to get feedback.

The second strategy for figuring out market-based pricing is to check out organizations who hire consultants to execute their programs. These are often higher-education programs, nonprofits, and foundations that support schools and districts. These organizations typically contract 20 to 30 consultants that they deploy to their school and district partners. Because they are hiring consultants in "bulk," they often have a standard pay scale. For example, one of my earliest consulting contracts was with a higher-education program that would send teams of three to four consultants to conduct site visits to their district partners. We were each paid $2,000 a day plus travel costs. While you don't have to price your site visits the same way, knowing the price of similar offers can be an interesting data point to help inform your market-based pricing.

These types of daily rates can be found for things like fellowship programs. If there are programs that you know of in the education space, go search their websites. You could also search on job sites like LinkedIn or Indeed for education consultant postings. Search the word *facilitator*, filter the search criteria for remote-work and contractor roles, and then start looking at those listings. You're gonna get an idea of what people are paying consultants by day, or by workshop, or by session. That's good data for your market-based pricing.

The third strategy is to review the pricing of your competitors. Now, when I say "competitors," I mean that loosely, 'cause your biggest competition is yourself, but you can research how other people in the marketplace value their work. You could look within education or outside of it. For example, if you are thinking of offering a virtual workshop, doing some research around other people who host workshops even if their expertise is outside education can be useful. Do a little digging to find out what folks who are offering similar services—whether that's a workshop or a PD session or a virtual training—are charging.

The final strategy is putting together a pre-consultation survey. Before you hop on a consultation or a discovery call with anyone, you should always have them complete a survey. And in the survey, one of your questions needs to be "What is your budget for this project?" In my own business, I wasn't direct enough at first and had to tweak this question because people were avoiding giving a real answer. But everybody has a budget. I don't care what they say. The amount someone is willing to pay to solve their problem might be in a spreadsheet somewhere, or just in their head, but it exists.

Like we've talked about at other points in the book, market-based pricing is something you will experiment with over time. That's okay and, honestly, should be expected. After all, flat-screens had to adjust too.

VALUE-BASED PRICING

The second approach puts a price tag on what your clients can expect to gain (or save) from working with you. The easiest way to explain value-based pricing is to use an example from an industry where gains are easy to monetize: manufacturing. Let's say a CEO of a product-based brand decides to hire an expert to optimize how they get products from the factory floor into stores. The consultant they hire has a proven history of saving companies over $50,000, which makes their $25,000 fee a no-brainer. Similarly, if the work you do regularly saves school districts $10,000, setting your fee at $5,000 makes your services easy to say yes to. The schools you work with get both a return on their investment and the result you offer at the same time.

The challenge in value-based pricing is that you have to articulate the financial value of your services in a way potential clients will understand. This approach puts the emphasis on the value of your expertise rather than accessibility or affordability. That's why the clearer you can be on the value of your services, the more effective this approach will be. And when you realize the tremendous return your clients can get—financially and otherwise—from working with you, you'll be more confident in your pricing and offers.

In many ways, a value-based approach to pricing is the opposite of a market-based one. Rather than prioritizing accessibility and volume, value-based pricing charges a premium. Instead of working with everyone, you are giving exclusive access to only a few clients and working with them more in depth. Because you're likely to go deeper in the content and provide a hands-on experience and more access to your expertise, value-based pricing works best for Tier 2 and Tier 3 offers.

A great example of value-based pricing is Apple. A new iPhone is typically $1,000+ compared to Android devices that sell for $500 to $800. Similarly, a new MacBook Pro costs anywhere from $1,400 to $2,600 compared to a range of $1,000 to $2,100 for similar PCs. In addition to their products feeling upscale in terms of design and quality, Apple makes all their products work seamlessly together. When you buy a MacBook, an iPhone, and AirPods, everything syncs together easily. Apple can charge more than its competitors, knowing that the *value* of a seamless experience resonates with its customers.

Within education consulting, you often see premium pricing in offers like PD. A great example is my friend Jalen's work. He specializes in education leadership with an anti-racism lens. Jalen charges $10,000 per person for a weeklong institute teaching his methodology. Now, if you're a school or district wrestling with how to equip your staff to lead from an anti-racist lens, what is that transformation worth? Think about the cost of not addressing racism: turnover, community mistrust, student harm. Suddenly, $10,000 feels less like a line item and more like an investment. That's the essence of value-based pricing—you're not charging for your time; you're charging for the result and the ripple effect it creates.

What I want you to notice is that with far fewer clients, Jalen can generate the same amount of revenue as the person offering a $200 workshop. Because the prices are higher with a value-based approach, he earns more revenue with every sale. However, in order for value-based pricing to work, Jalen has to help his potential customers understand the value of that $10,000 workshop through effective marketing.

That's why you need to be really clear on the value that you're providing for your clients when you use this approach. The focus is on the value of what you provide, and showing that what you charge is just a fraction of what your clients or customers will get in return for their investment. To begin figuring out what the value of your service is, consider how much it would cost your TCF to alleviate their pain points and ultimately solve the problem as you would. Include the financial investments, the time spent (and wasted), and the opportunity cost of not hiring someone with your expertise and genius.

TIER-BASED PRICING

The best thing about market-based and value-based pricing is that these approaches can coexist within your business. While you can use both, you want to be strategic. Using market-based pricing is useful for your Tier 0 and Tier 1 offers because those are meant to be your most affordable and high-volume offers, whereas value-based pricing is appropriate for Tier 2 and Tier 3 offers, which are more exclusive and more intensive, and therefore cost more. After working with hundreds of education consultants and being an entrepreneur in the game for more than a minute, I can share a rough range of where your pricing can be for each of these tiers.

Please know that these ranges are guidelines. What I'm about to share are the prices you want to be striving toward. If you feel uncomfortable or anything less than confident about these ranges, you can pick a lower starting point and work your way up. But trust me when I say that when people have a problem, they will pay for a solution that works. And that's exactly what you are showing up with.

If you serve individuals (B2C)

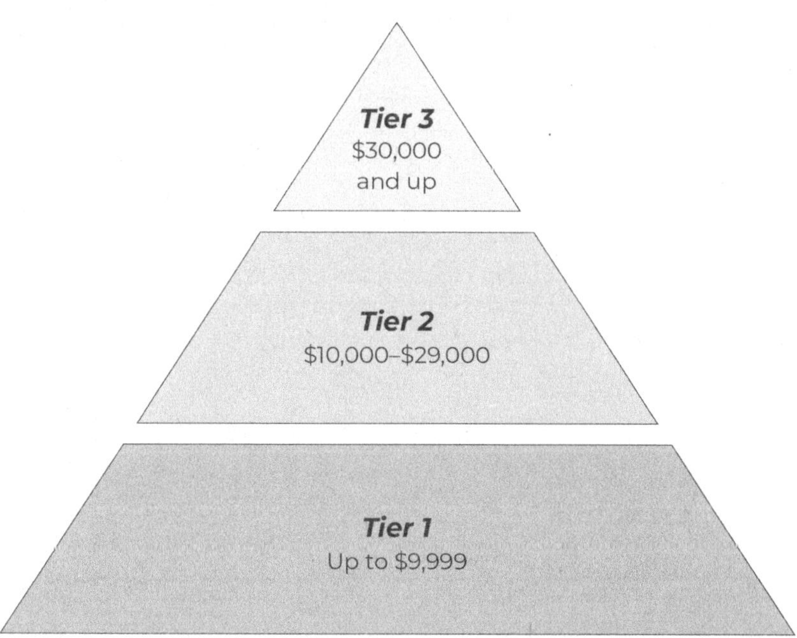

As mentioned earlier, a B2C model is when your contract is with an individual client. This model can also include sponsorship, which is when an organization like a school district or a nonprofit pays on behalf of the individual you are contracting with.

Suggested price ranges for the B2C model:

Tier 1 offer is up to $9,999

Tier 2 is $10,000 to $29,000

Tier 3 offer is $30,000 and up

If you serve organizations and businesses (including nonprofits and school districts):

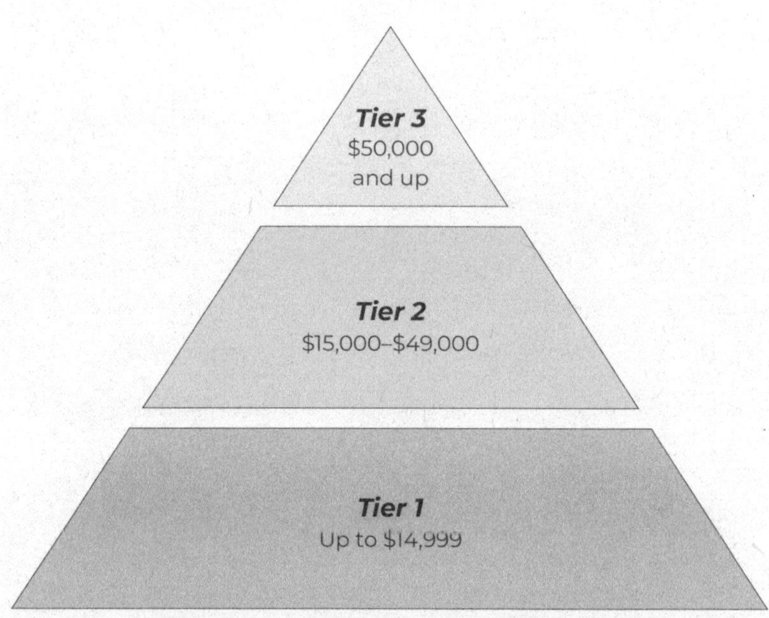

As a reminder, you are in a B2B model when your contract is with an organization.

Suggested price ranges for the B2B model:

Tier 1 offer is up to $14,999

Tier 2 is $15,000 to $49,000

Tier 3 offer is $50,000 and up

Looking at these ranges, maybe your heart started beating fast, or you thought, *There's no way someone can afford to pay that much*, or *Oh my gosh, I can't ask for that*. That's okay.

Remember, these ranges are all recommendations. You can work up to these prices. As I said before, people pay to solve problems they see as insurmountable.

Especially when you have solutions that are driven by previous Receipts, Experience, and a unique Skill set. (Notice what I did there?) There is always a way, but I share these ranges with you so that you can see what's already being paid for this kind of work, what education consultants like you are getting right now. This transparency around pricing is important, because educators like us tend to default to the idea that we should accept less money because we love what we do. But that's wrong and only keeps us from building the wealth we deserve.

RUN YOUR NUMBERS

Let's walk through a strategy that combines everything you've learned in this chapter into actual pricing you can use in your business. Before we jump in, I want you to repeat after me: "We are all math people." Say it one more time, with a little more bass in your voice: "We are all math people." Let's touch and agree and jump into it!

We are going to start by figuring out what you need to earn to cover your expenses, both for your business and for your personal life, because making that money is what your business is for. Yes, you are going to make an impact. Yes, you are going to do terrific work. But you're also doing this to get paid, to generate freedom, and to create intergenerational wealth. This strategy starts with that in mind. I want you to plan carefully, because for any pricing to work, you have to actually *make* money. You need to make enough money to both pay your expenses and take care of your own needs. That's a nonnegotiable.

That's why your first task will be to figure out how much money you need every month to cover *all* your expenses. Once you have that number, divide it by the number of hours every month that you can dedicate to your business. That could be 40 to 60 hours per month if your business is part-time (that's 10 to 15 hours weekly) or 140 to 160 hours if you're full-time (35 to 40 hours weekly). This will give you a rough hourly rate. While we don't use an hourly rate to determine pricing, I do find this helpful as a starting point.

Let's walk through an example. My client Brianna needs $4,000 to cover her bills and personal expenses and another $1,000 to cover business expenses, for a total of $5,000 a month. She wants to quit her job, but in the meantime, she's working every weekend on her new business. After tracking her time, Brianna estimates she averages ~25 hours working on her business per month. Her math would be $5,000 divided by 25, so her hourly rate would be $200.

Don't forget Uncle Sam

In my pricing formula, I always include a 25 percent add-on for taxes. Let's be clear, this number isn't exact. It's a conservative baseline that gives you a cushion so you're not caught off guard when tax season comes. The truth is, your actual tax percentage will depend on your income, your deductions, and your business structure.

If you want to know the exact number you should plan around, this is where a good accountant comes in. Taxes are too important to leave to guesswork. My 25 percent add-on is about building discipline into your pricing so you're prepared, but your accountant can help you tailor that number to your specific situation.

An hourly rate gives you a baseline to begin to calculate your offer pricing. When I met her, Brianna wanted to start her business by offering half-day PD sessions for new teachers. While it might seem like the price is obvious (her hourly rate times a half day), that rate doesn't account for her expenses, aka her cost to deliver that PD. She needs to put a value on her prep time, the cost of supplies, perhaps any travel time or expenses associated with getting to the PD session, and any follow-up that's needed.

BRIANNA'S HALF PD DAY COSTS

Her hourly rate for the actual session ($200 x 4) =	*$800*
Prep time ($200 x 5 hours) =	*$1,000*
Cost of supplies =	*$100*
Travel time (1 hour) and cost (gas, mileage, etc.) =	*$300*
Follow-up ($200 x 2 hours) =	*$400*
TOTAL	*$2,600*

But wait, that's not all.

There is also an optional "bug-a-boo" tax of 15 percent that I calculate into pricing to account for the inevitable time that you'll have to spend handling a bug-a-boo. If you wanna change your bug-a-boo tax (or remove it entirely), that's on you, but a bug-a-boo tax covers that one needy client who takes up time asking a million questions. You know the one. They text, saying, "Hey, can we hop on the phone real quick?" Or shoot you an e-mail a month after your workshop: "Can you review this for me?" Or ask for additional support here and there beyond the agreed-upon scope of work. Rather than getting annoyed by the extra work (and telling MCI to cut the phone poles), I just bake it into the price up front so I can serve without resentment.

And last, you want to add in a profit margin of at least 50 percent. Your profit margin is how much money your business gets to "keep" after all your costs are paid. As a service-based business, the minimum profit margin you want to include is 30 percent, though you could reasonably go up to 50 percent. Remember, we're not in business to break even.

Let's revisit Brianna's PD session:

So, $4,940 would be the minimum Brianna should charge for a half day of PD. Note that this is still a Tier 1 offer in both the B2B and B2C models.

Let's do another example with Brianna for her Tier 2 offer. For a Tier 2 offer, Brianna decides to run a series of three half-day PD sessions with in-person coaching between sessions.

BRIANNA'S TIER 2 OFFER

Her hourly rate for 3 half-day PD sessions =	**$2,400**
Her hourly rate for 2 coaching sessions =	**$400**
Prep time ($200 x 17 hours) =	**$3,400**
Cost of supplies (including a client gift) =	**$150**
Travel time and costs for 5 round-trips ($300 per round-trip) =	**$1,500**
Follow-up ($200 x 10 hours) =	**$2,000**
TOTAL	**$9,850**
+ bug-a-boo tax of 15% =	**$1,477.50**
+ taxes 25% =	**$2,462.50**
+ profit margin 50% =	**$4,925**
PRICE	**$18,715**

You can use this same formula with all the different pricing approaches and for every offer you come up with. Now that you understand how to do this, I want to address a couple of the questions I get when I teach this approach to my clients. I've taught this a lot, so I know that you are wondering whether you can offer a group discount.

Know this: Whenever you decide to reduce prices for any reason, you're cutting into your profit margin. That's okay every once in a while, but your profit margin is both your financial buffer (so you can build reserves) and your personal income as the owner of the business. Now, there could be a time when you tell someone your price, like Brianna's $18,715 for her Tier 2 offer, and they respond by saying their budget is $15,000. Because you know your numbers, you might be able to say, okay, I have that wiggle room. You could:

- cut your profit margin from 50 percent to 30 percent, reducing your profit; or
- remove the two coaching sessions, which would have required two hours of prep time and two round-trips of travel, reducing the expenses.

BRIANNA'S ADJUSTED TIER 2 OFFER
FOR A $15K BUDGET

Her hourly rate for 3 half-day PD sessions =	**$2,400**
Prep time ($200 x 15 hours) =	**$3,000**
Cost of supplies (including a client gift) =	**$150**
Travel time and costs for 3 round-trips ($300 per round-trip) =	**$900**
Follow-up ($200 x 10 hours) =	**$2,000**

TOTAL	**$8,450**
+bug-a-boo tax of 15% =	**$1,267.50**
+ taxes 25% =	**$2,112.50**
+ profit margin 30% =	**$2,535**

PRICE	**$14,365**

These adjustments reduce the package to $14,365. Brianna is still able to pay herself $7,400, cover all her expenses, and make a profit of $2,535, not including the bug-a-boo tax. She could also do fewer reductions and counter the client to try to meet in the middle at $16,000 or $17,000. Either way, running the numbers lets her know that both scenarios still allow her to make money.

What you want to avoid is completely sacrificing your profit margin in order to land a client, because that puts stress on you and your business. Another lesson in the hidden curriculum of entrepreneurship is that not all money is good money. When you use my pricing formula to get real clarity on your numbers, you can prevent that stress from happening.

PRICING IS A JOURNEY

Setting prices always presents complexities because we each have our own experiences with money. However, in this chapter I've given you resources to help you triangulate your data so that you can make the best decision for you. That's a callback to questions like "how did you triangulate your data" when we as educators would assess student achievement or metrics or multiple points of view. I want you to take a similar rigorous and multifaceted approach to your pricing.

In this chapter, I've given you multiple data points that will allow you to experiment with pricing for your offers. That includes the three approaches to pricing that you can combine to complement the 7-FigurED Offer framework you learned in Chapter 5 and the examples of how to run your numbers. Collectively this gives you the data you need to pick a starting point for how you'll price your offers.

I know the ranges and information and examples I've given may feel scary, but what I've offered are just guidelines. For some of you, the prices I've outlined may be prices you strive for, because you feel uncomfortable with that number *today*. There's a fine line between choosing a number that might be a reach and pushing too far outside your comfort zone. If you do not feel confident about the price you've decided to set for an offer, if there's any part of you that is wavering or doubtful when you speak it out loud, don't use that price.

In other words: Don't choose a price because you read it in a book, m'kay? If you do that and you aren't 100 percent confident, you're creating an invisible roadblock. You're going to feel nervous or uncertain, and clients will pick up on that. You will receive more nos than yeses and wonder why, when it is because your potential clients couldn't feel confident in you because they sensed *you* didn't feel confident in you. Your clients need to hear your confidence in order to say yes. In fact, some of your clients are going to need to borrow your conviction to make their next move. That's why it's so important that you feel comfortable and ready to stand by your prices. Please remember that what you choose today in terms of pricing your offers doesn't have to be permanent; nor does it have to be exactly within the ranges I've shared.

Set a price today that you can feel confident about and that feels like a little bit of a stretch. That may be $3,000. That may be $15,000. Or maybe it's $30,000. Whatever that number is, you are going to get that contract, show up, do the work, and slay (as you do), and the number may sound different to you. That same number is going to sound different the day you get a raving testimonial talking about how transformative and impactful your services are. And then you're going to get to a point where you think something like, *Wow,*

I did slay this. I think I'm going to raise that price. And maybe you'll get a contract for that same offer at $6,000 or $30,000 or $60,000. You'll show up and slay again, get more glowing testimonials again, and hear those numbers differently again. Soon you'll find yourself thinking, *I get amazing results. I should charge more.*

That, my friends, is the journey of pricing you're going to go on.

CHAPTER 7 REFLECTION QUESTIONS

1. What money mindsets will you need to manage as you set your pricing?

2. What price point could you say with your chest today? What is the price threshold that makes you feel a little nervous?

3. Which approach to pricing, market based or value based, are you most attracted to as a consumer, and why? Which approach are you more attracted to as a business owner, and why?

4. Consider the tiered offers you created in Chapter 5. Do you want to use a market-based approach or a value-based approach to pricing for each of your offers?

ACTION STEPS

- Survey your TCFs (if you haven't already) about pricing.
    - Similarly, if you do consult or discovery calls, be sure to send those prospects a survey asking about pricing/budget prior to the call.
- Run your numbers.
- Set the initial pricing for each of your offers (and remember to adjust as you show up and slay).

7-FIGURE EDUCATOR RESOURCES

Visit **www.7febook.com/resources** to:

- Download my guide for Inclusive Pricing
- Review Nathan Barry's "Ladders of Wealth Creation" article
- Watch Episode 4: "6 Figures in a Quarter: What's Your Excuse?" of the *7-Figure Educator* podcast, where I sit down with a member of our community, Erinn Cottman, to learn more about her journey in evolving her pricing to achieve a six-figure quarter in her business
- Watch Episode 48: "3 Things Millionaires Know About Success That You Don't" of the *7 Figure Educator* podcast to continue to unpack the mindset work that will impact your pricing

Flex Your Funnel

*Objective: To generate 50 or more
potential clients in your business*

Brittany was struggling in her business when she found me on social media. As a former principal, teacher, peer mediator, and positive behavioral interventions and supports (PBIS) coordinator for her school district, Brittany had tons of experience in education and the receipts to show it. Starting her education consulting business felt like a natural step when she was looking for more flexibility and more income, and that's exactly what she did in 2012. Brittany put in the work and grew her business to over six figures in annual revenue, but she wasn't happy. One issue was that all her contracts were customized work. Can somebody say "Tier 3"? She had no Tier 1 or Tier 2 clients. While that may not sound like a problem on the surface, this meant that she had no rinse-and-repeatable services. Every new client required creating all new systems because the work was not the same. In addition, all her contracts were underpriced. So, she was caught in the same overworked-and-underpaid cycle she had tried to leave behind at her district job. When your six figures are this hard, the thought of seven figures will make your chest tight. And to top it off, Brittany was relying on referrals, which meant she had no marketing strategy and therefore, no control of her revenue. She had to wait on the next referral in order to make more money.

By the time she ran into one of my videos on YouTube nearly a decade after founding her business, Brittany was exhausted. She didn't want to be so dependent on referrals. She was tired of re-creating her services every time a new client came on board or a district changed their mind. And, like many educators, Brittany wanted a better lifestyle—and to get that, her business needed to make more money.

Brittany had previously tried to host a webinar as a way to get new clients. On that webinar, she taught good content and thought she had left the door open for attendees to reach out to her if they were interested in working together. While the webinar had strong turnout, nothing happened afterward. Brittany had assumed that if people were interested in hiring her, they would follow up on their own. But there was nothing. Zero sales. No new clients. Not even a complimentary thank-you e-mail in her inbox. Brittany was puzzled. It wasn't until Brittany joined Wealthy Black Educator, my mastermind program, that she realized what she had done wrong.

Brittany had unintentionally taught a workshop. She had delivered great content and actionable advice . . . but failed to include a concrete way for the attendees to work with her afterward. She didn't make a formal pitch for her services. There was no call to action. People didn't follow up, because she didn't actually offer to continue the conversation the webinar had started.

Flash forward to a webinar Brittany hosted after she had worked with me and my team in my mastermind program. After putting into action what I'm about to teach you, Brittany got over 100 people to register and landed two new five-figure contracts. Today, she's well on her way to building a seven-figure business with a clear marketing strategy that generates clients rather than waiting on the next referral.

In this chapter I'm going to show you how to do the same by building relationships through systematic touchpoints that allow you to qualify potential clients and create opportunities for you to sell your services. Let's address the elephant in the room before we get started. We are going to talk about sales in this chapter. And to some of you, that might feel like a scary word. But the reality is that you have to sell in your business in order to have a business. If you don't sell, you don't have a business; you have a hobby. A lot of people have a fear of being "salesy" and do their best to avoid that used-car-salesman, laying-it-on-thick vibe. I get it. We've all had an experience of being sold to in a sleazy, pressure-filled, uncomfortable way. I'm not going to ask you to do that, because that's the opposite of an effective sales strategy. Any salesperson who jumps immediately to the pitch and the purchase is going to make you feel uncomfortable because there's zero trust built and zero relationship. That's not good business.

EVERYONE IS A SALESPERSON

You've already been selling. We just use different terminology in education. If you've ever said that you were going to get "buy-in" from your district or your principal or your staff or even from your spouse and children—you've done sales. It's just helping people make a decision that's in their best interest. If you've ever convinced your friends to stay out at the club for one more round—or that y'all really need to call that car, like, *now*—you've had a successful sales conversation. We assume that "sales" has to resemble a time-share presentation or those folks who corner you on the street, asking you to donate to a charity. But in reality, "sales" can be as simple as providing help, showing that you understand someone's problem, and continuing the conversation.

Sales is simply a conversation between you and your TCF where you *help* them make a decision. When you realize the focus is on your potential client, you understand that selling is helping. In any sales conversation, your objective is to share how your business solves their problem. A lot of times, we let how we think we'll be perceived hold us back from making a sales pitch for our services. But how dare you keep a solution you know is going to work from someone, solely for the protection of your own ego? Do you think so highly of yourself that you're not willing to take a chance in order to help someone else out? Of course it is icky and maybe even morally questionable to sell products and services to people who don't really need our help. But I'm not advocating you do that.

Instead, what you are going to learn is how to start conversations and show up in a way that will help your TCF understand how they can succeed. How you can solve their problem. How your services can fulfill and maybe surpass their expectations and needs. How you can continue to be in relationship until, like Brittany's clients, they trust you enough to give you some of their hard-earned money (or budget) in exchange for solving their problems.

I'm going to show you how to build the kind of relationship with your TCFs where they trust you to thoughtfully and ethically provide a solution to a problem you know they have. I can't guarantee you will always feel comfortable, especially if you are new to actively selling, but I can guarantee that you'll be selling from a spirit of service because you've been building a relationship with your client throughout the whole process. My 7-FigurED Sales Funnel will help ensure that the people you have sales conversations with will be the absolute right fit for your business.

Last, I'm going to help you get started right now both within your network and in the broader online world with a challenge to generate 50 or more potential clients within your business in the next 30 days. That might seem like a lot, but it's entirely possible. Let's go.

BUILD YOUR 7-FIGURED SALES FUNNEL

Get excited, because this is the moment where we turn all the work you've done so far into paid clients. I'm going to show you how to build a "funnel," which is a fancy word for the path potential clients take from knowing you exist to making a purchase. But even more importantly, your funnel is an intentional road map for how to nurture your audience, build a relationship with the people who enter your ecosystem, and create trust over time so that you are attracting right-fit clients who will spend money with you.

A funnel in business looks a lot like the funnel you may remember from the science lab at school. The largest part is at the top and as you move down, the funnel gets narrower, with the smallest part at the bottom. In your business, the number of TCFs at the top of your funnel is significantly larger than the number of TCFs at the bottom—who become paying clients. Even with great messaging and targeted marketing, not everyone you attract is going to be the right fit. That's to be expected. After all, not every friend you make ends up a bestie in a Tessie, and that's okay.

I am going to teach you my 7-FigurED Sales Funnel through two perspectives. First, we will review the funnel through the lens of *a relationship*. I'm going to use a dating analogy here to show you how a relationship funnel works in real life. Because you do have to date your audience. You need to show up consistently and be dependable. When you post one time on social media and expect people to buy, that's the equivalent of sending someone you're interested in a text that says "wyd" and expecting them to respond, "Put a ring on it pooh." Not gonna happen.

The disconnect is in the approach. In business, like in romance, you need to build a relationship for anybody to feel good about locking anything down. That's what I'm going to teach you how to do. As we move through the steps of this relationship-building process, notice: How is your relationship with the potential client evolving? Once I show you the stages of the relationship, we can move to the sales strategy that helps move that relationship forward.

Let's first start with looking at your 7-FigurED Sales Funnel from the relationship perspective of getting to know your audience and creating trust. There are four stages to a relationship funnel:

1. Awareness

2. Consideration

3. Preference

4. Purchase

RELATIONSHIP FUNNEL

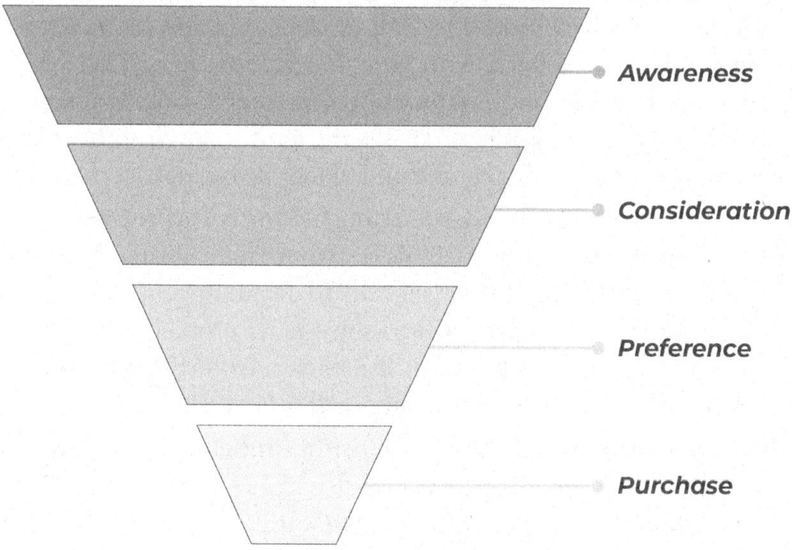

Awareness is when you create content with the sole intention of attracting attention; of letting folks know that you exist. In the dating analogy, this is where you create a dating app profile with that cute pic from your last vacation. Just like you can't get chosen without a profile, a client can't buy from you if they don't know who you are. You must build awareness of your business. Research shows that the average adult attention span has shrunk from 150 seconds in 2004 to 47 seconds or less as of 2023. And that can be even shorter on social media platforms or with sponsored content like ads. Luckily, you've already done the work to understand what your TCF is experiencing and know the language to use in your content to attract their attention (as we talked about in Chapter 6). By focusing on the problem and employing the same language they use to describe it, your TCF is going to feel like you understand them from the jump.

Consideration is the next step in your funnel.

At this point, your TCF knows who you are and has gained a deeper understanding of their problem by engaging with your content. Now your TCF is looking for possible solutions and is curious about how you might be able to help them solve their problem. This is the equivalent of someone swiping right on your profile and seeing if you match.

The third stage in your relationship funnel is **Preference**.

This is when your TCF moves from "maybe they might know what they are talking about" to deciding you would be a great person to work with to solve their problem. Or, like when your casual dates with the person from the app turn into a conversation about seeing each other exclusively.

At this point in your relationship funnel, they are clear on wanting to work with you, but you as a business owner also get to decide whether or not you want to work with them. You get to qualify whether each individual organization or person has a problem that you can actually solve.

And the last step in a relationship funnel is **Purchase**.

This stage is pretty obvious: It's when you have built up enough trust and rapport with a TCF that they go from someone who doesn't know you, to someone who is intrigued, to someone who wants to work with you, to someone who signs a contract and pays. The dating equivalent here would be defining the relationship and deciding to go together real bad.

The dating analogy is a good reminder that not everyone is going to make it to this point, but having people who do is a good sign your funnel is effective in building a relationship with your TCF. Now let's revisit our same relationship funnel through the second perspective of sales strategy.

Awareness = Traffic Generation

Consideration = Lead Generation

Preference = Prospect Generation

Purchase = Client Conversion

7-FIGURED™ FUNNEL

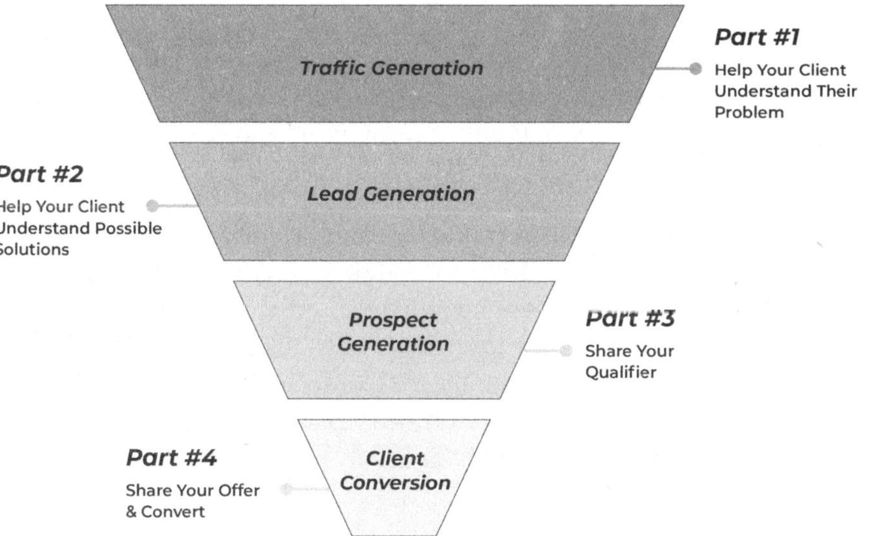

AWARENESS = TRAFFIC GENERATION

Traffic measures the number of people who land on your marketing assets (social media account, website, landing page, checkout, webinar registration page, etc.) during a period of time. This is the very top of your funnel, meaning you're aiming for as much traffic as you can get. At this stage the goal is to generate attention. Content that resonates with how your TCF feels and helps them better understand their own problems is key. And because of the attention deficits in the marketplace I mentioned earlier, you also want to consider a mix of short-, mid-, and long-form content.

- Short-form content is quick and snackable. Think Instagram reels, Tik Toks, or a two-minute video.

- Mid-form content goes a bit deeper, like a LinkedIn post, a podcast episode snippet, or a blog under 1,000 words.

- Long-form content is where you really unpack ideas and flex your expertise, such as a full webinar, a YouTube training, or a detailed white paper.

You can also drive traffic through delivery of in-person workshops, talks, and keynotes that showcase the problem your TCF experiences at conferences and seminars that you know your TCF is likely to attend. The traffic-generation stage is where all the work you did in Chapter 6 begins to pay off, because you know where and how to show up so the TCFs who need help know that you deeply understand them and their problem.

CONSIDERATION = LEAD GENERATION

Now that you have people following you or interacting with your content, how can you determine who is actually interested in learning more? That's where lead generation comes in. A lead is a person or business that has expressed interest in what you have to offer, usually by giving you their e-mail address. Leads are still near the top of your funnel, because you are both still getting to know one another. Most of the time, you don't know whether a lead is exactly your TCF or not.

To generate leads, you want to give people the opportunity to learn more by "opting in" to hear from or receive something from you on a regular basis. The goal is to provide something valuable enough for your TCF to want to give you their e-mail address. Most of the time, that requires creating a "lead magnet." Note that your opt-in ask needs to be sexier than "opt in to my list" or "get my free newsletter." It's not enough to offer a weekly e-mail in exchange for their contact information. Instead, you're going to offer a free resource, or lead magnet, that helps to solve a piece of their problem.

There are three different subtypes within the broader umbrella of leads: cold, warm, and hot. Each type requires a different approach within your funnel and overall approach to sales and marketing.

Your **cold** leads are people who've never heard of you or your services, ever. When these folks hear your name, you are a stranger. They don't know you, which is why they're cold.

Your **warm** leads are people who've been exposed to you and your business services, and maybe they've shown some interest. Perhaps they follow you on social media, or maybe they are on your e-mail list or simply visited your website. There's some context and familiarity but a lot of opportunity to know you and your business more deeply.

And then there's your **hot** leads. These are the folks who sign up as soon as you open doors on a new offer or ask them to renew. Your hot audience can include past and existing clients, past colleagues, or organizations that you've had the opportunity to work with before. This could include folks from your 9-to-5 who deeply know your work, like your previous boss. Your hot audience has been witness to your genius and has engaged with some version of your service before. We call them hot because they're the folks who are most likely to convert to paid clients since there is already trust established.

They don't need to be convinced of how great you are, because they already know.

While all lead generation is important, it's a heightened priority to engage with your hot and warm audiences (particularly when you are pre-revenue), because those are the people who are most likely to convert. They're the low-hanging fruit, the quick wins that will come because those folks already know you got the sauce. Existing relationships allow you to leapfrog multiple steps in the sales process. When you're focused on serving your warm and hot audiences first, you don't have to worry about generating traffic and creating awareness, because those folks already know you exist. And you don't have to work at converting these audiences to become leads, because you likely already have their contact information. While you may not have their e-mail address, you might be able to DM them on social media and get a response. When you start by nurturing your warm and hot leads, you don't have to do as much relationship building, because you already know each other.

Now I know what you're thinking: *That's all well and good, Erica, but what do I do to reach my cold audience?* We're going to get to that in the next chapter, because reaching new folks requires more strategy. I am intentionally slowing your roll and encouraging you to put in your reps on your hot and warm audiences first. That will allow you to test how you're showing up with a more receptive audience so that you can be even more successful later on. In business, like in life, patience and practice are key.

HOW TO CREATE AND
LEVERAGE A LEAD MAGNET

To help you understand how lead magnets work, let's walk through a common strategy.

My client Alicia helps new school leaders thrive in their new roles by offering both one-on-one and group coaching. She generates *awareness* by creating social media content around the pain points of her TCF. When sharing her content, she teases a link to a PDF guide to "5 Mindset Shifts Teachers Need to Make When They Become School Leaders." To receive that PDF guide, Alicia's followers need to provide their names and e-mail addresses. That PDF guide is her lead magnet.

You can also create and use paid lead magnets. Here's a great example: As an expert in special education, my client Derek is asked to do a lot of presentations at conferences. His presentation is not a lead magnet; instead, it's an awareness strategy. He uses the presentation to talk about the problem that his TCF faces. After demonstrating that he understands their problems, Derek tells his audiences that he has an upcoming paid workshop. If folks are interested, they can enter their e-mail to sign up. That paid workshop—even though it's paid—is his lead magnet.

The big thing to recognize is that while you generate *awareness* by talking about the pain points and the problem your TCF experiences, your lead magnet offers *value* through providing a micro-solution to a micro-version of their problem. In fact, the best lead magnets offer a "quick win" for your TCF that builds trust and moves them to the next stage of your relationship funnel: Preference.

PREFERENCE = PROSPECT GENERATION

At this point, you've done the work to make sure people know you exist (awareness/traffic), and some of those people have given you their contact information (consideration/lead generation). Now you get to create a way to qualify your leads and confirm a mutual fit for your services. Unfortunately, not every lead will be qualified to work with you. Evaluating the quality of your leads is an important step that a lot of people skip. If you've ever had a discovery call with a lead where they said they didn't have the budget for your services, you didn't qualify properly, because you should have known that information *before* they booked the call.

The goal is to qualify folks based on the characteristics you outlined in your TCF profile in Chapter 6. Qualifiers could include requiring folks to fill out a survey prior to booking a consultation or discovery call. (Pro tip: If you do this, make sure that budget is one of the questions you ask.) A quiz or assessment could also be a potential qualifier. Another option would be to have a paid offer at this point in your funnel. I am talking a low-ticket price point, so under $100. The goal isn't to make money off the qualifier but instead to identify who the serious buyers are. Earlier I talked about my client Brittany. Her qualifier could be charging $48 for her webinar. You could do a paid discovery call that has a $25 deposit. (Pro tip: If you decide to make your qualifier paid, you can apply the cost of your qualifier as a credit toward a client's fee if they decide to move forward.) The objective at this stage is to determine which of your leads are *prospects*—individuals or businesses that truly match your TCF profile (or come very close) and qualify for your services. Keep in mind that because prospect generation is further down the funnel, you will have fewer prospects than leads. That's normal.

PURCHASE = CLIENT CONVERSION

So, you've generated traffic. (Awareness)

Then you have some of those people saying, "I'm interested, I wanna learn more," and giving you their e-mail in exchange for a piece of your expertise. (Consideration)

You have used a qualifier to identify who would be a good fit. (Preference)

And now we're talking *conversion*: getting people to buy your offer. (Purchase)

At this point, you are making a formal offer to work together. This could be through pitching the offer on a sales call or at the end of a webinar, or sending a proposal. Whatever format you use, you want to do more than just explain the details of your offer. You also want to address all the objections you identified while making your TCF profile in Chapter 6. Rather than wait for someone to say "I can't afford it" or "I have to think about it," address those from the jump. Use your R-E-S, use your social proof, use your testimonials to make the decision a no-brainer, because it *is* a no-brainer.

Because when you do your funnel right, you already have the trust of your TCF. They're on the phone, or on Zoom, or attending the webinar because they trust you and want to work with you. The opportunity is there. You know you can help, so make the offer and land the contract.

Conferences: don't just teach; convert

For education consultants, conferences are one of the most common ways to build awareness of your business. But here's the mistake most people make: They show up ready to teach, deliver a strong session, and then leave the room hoping attendees will somehow follow up on their own.

That's not how this works.

If you're serious about building relationships, you need to give your Target Client Friend (TCF) a clear next step. Don't just end with a thank-you; end with a call to action. Maybe that's inviting them to sign up for a free resource, join your e-mail list, or attend your webinar the following week. Even if the conference restricts selling or pitching, you can still give a call to action that allows you to continue to nurture the relationship—like, "Sign up to get the handouts from this session."

Remember: Conferences aren't just about awareness. They're also your chance to invite people into consideration, where they raise their hand and say "I want to hear more from you."

THE REMIX

I want to take a second to recap what you just learned, because as educators we all know that sometimes you have to explain the same lesson a couple different ways before everybody in the room picks up what you're putting down.

So. Here's the 7-FigurED funnel explained from another angle. People cannot and will not purchase unless they are first aware of you. Your marketing and branding (which we'll address in the next chapter) are how you build that awareness of your services and of who you are. People cannot become loyal, or renew, or share their results with friends and colleagues, without first becoming aware of who you are.

From awareness, you have to start building a relationship and creating trust, because once again, you're basically a stranger. By providing your folks with a quick win through a lead magnet, you create even more trust. Some of those people are going to take the next step and show interest in working with you, which is when you're going to present them with a qualifier.

This can be a quiz, a pre-consult survey, or a discovery call. The point of your qualifying step is to separate who you work with and who you don't so that you make offers only to people who are a good fit to actually work with you.

Then once you've identified who is a fit for your services, you make an offer. This can be a verbal pitch on a webinar or a written pitch through sending a proposal. It's not good enough to qualify folks and expect them to reach out on their own. You must make a formal invite to work with you.

Put all together, the 7-FigurED funnel is a systematized way to build your audience, generate leads and prospects, and make offers.

Most people don't buy right away

Only 2 percent of people buy at the first opportunity.

Instead, most people need 14 to 20 touchpoints to spend money.

Consider: Did you buy this book the first time you heard about it? Did you pay to learn from me the first time you were given a chance? Maybe you did and are one of the 2 percent, but that's statistically unlikely. What I see all the time is folks expecting their customers to buy off a single social media post when it took them two years to buy from a fellow entrepreneur (me).

If you don't even move that way, don't expect others to. Instead, focus on creating trust and building the relationship through multiple touchpoints, like I mentioned before. Going back to our dating analogy from earlier in the chapter, each of those touchpoints is like a text from your future boo. *How is your day? I'd love to see you this weekend. I had a fun time last night on our date.* Because all those small moments build trust and move you forward—and maybe you eventually put a ring on it.

THE IMPORTANCE OF EXPERIMENTATION

Mikenna was so excited about her webinar. She had done everything I told you to do so far in this chapter, and 20 people had signed up. But on the actual day of the webinar, no one showed up. Mikenna felt embarrassed but was also grateful, she said later, that no one saw her fail so badly. She was convinced that this was the end of her business.

Y'all, I hate to break it to you, but your funnel may not work perfectly the first time. Like with so many of the strategies I've provided in this book, I want you to approach your funnel with a sense of experimentation and curiosity. A creative way to approach this work is to treat your funnel the same way you approached student mastery when you were in the classroom. When I taught geometry, I didn't expect all my students to understand a new concept on day one. Instead, I would teach a lesson—say, the properties of right triangles—and then measure how many students understood. That became my baseline, and from there I could experiment. I could try group work. I could try homework assignments. I could try different approaches and continue to give my students assessments until I got to a level of mastery I felt confident about.

If this reminds you of data-driven instruction (DDI), you get an A+. We all know that the best teachers (y'all included) collect data on everything they can. Just like when I taught geometry, when I teach my courses today, I always include a "Do Now" activity with two to three questions for my students to answer on a prerequisite topic. I know based on my students' answers to those questions if I need to do any quick reteaching before I jump into my lesson. Those answers give me immediate data to know in real time how to adjust. After all, I don't want to reteach a concept that everybody gets, and I also don't want to leave anyone behind who doesn't quite understand yet. If I see that folks aren't following, I am going to reteach. The same applies to funnels. Just like DDI, you're looking for the data at every stage of your funnel and sales process to adjust and refine how you operate.

I want to make sure you see the meta lesson in this example. As a teacher, I wasn't surprised when my first lesson didn't result in 100 percent mastery. After seeing that only a small number of my students understood right triangles on my first go, I didn't blame myself. I didn't suddenly decide that I was doomed to fail forever. Instead, I saw that first result as a baseline I could experiment with to test other approaches and to eventually get to mastery through reteaching and using data to iterate.

It makes total sense to feel embarrassed, ashamed, or even start to assume you're doomed to fail forever when you have an experience like Mikenna's. But an important part of entrepreneurship is not being afraid to be a beginner again, to try again, to start again. For educators, the natural parallel is taking on the perspective of a first-year teacher. In that role, most of us would say that we didn't know what we didn't know. That we were walking into experiences with the intention to learn. Making a similar shift in how you think about your funnel—and really, your whole business—will allow you to embrace entrepreneurship in a meaningful way. Your funnel is going to be a continual experiment. The funnel you design after reading this chapter? You're going to run that for at least 90 days. You're going to collect all the data you can at every stage of your funnel during that time. How much traffic are you generating? How many leads are signing up for your lead magnet? How many of your leads are qualified and become prospects? How many new clients or contracts did you get? This 90-day experiment is your baseline. Depending on your data, there may be obvious things that can be tweaked or changed.

The important thing is not to throw the whole funnel away without giving it the opportunity to work. You want to keep your data clean from iteration to iteration. The scientific method is just as useful for the funnel in your business as it is for the lab in your school. When you do decide to iterate, tweak only one aspect at a time so you can see in the data what changes. Also, keep your funnel simple. At each stage, there should be one strategy that all your traffic, all your leads, all your prospects interact with. That will make analyzing your data so much easier than if you have dozens of strategies working at the same time.

The goal of all this experimentation is predictability. For example, if I want five new clients in a given quarter, my funnel should be so tight, effective, and consistent that I can know exactly how many people I need to attract at the top (through traffic or leads) to end up with five new paying clients. To calculate that, you can work from the bottom up. Let's say I have 50 percent conversion at every stage of my funnel. Which means that as we move down the funnel, every stage has half the number of people as the stage above it (or, going bottom up, twice as many people at each stage as the one below it).

I start with my desired number of clients at the bottom of the funnel. The number of clients I want (five) times two means I need 10 people as prospects. I also have a 50 percent conversion from lead to prospect, so I would need twice the number of prospects (10), or 20 leads. And 50 percent of my overall traffic becomes a lead, so I do the same math—two times my 20 leads—to calculate that I need 40 people at the top of the funnel to get five clients in the end.

7-FIGURED™ FUNNEL

50% CONVERSION EXAMPLE

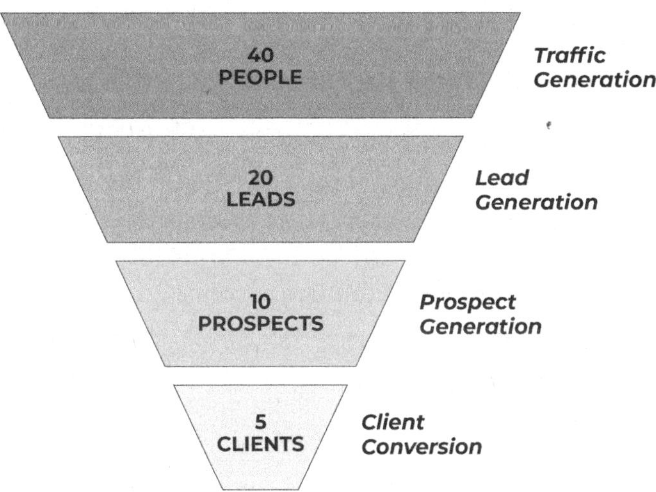

Keep in mind that when you're first starting out, you'll be working with warm and hot leads, which may mean that you have higher conversion rates compared to a cold audience because the people you're interacting with already know you. But you can still run this data even if you are generating leads through your network. Let's say you start by reaching out to 50 people. Keep track of your funnel: How many people respond to your content? How many go from lead to prospect? How many sales conversations do you have? How many new clients or contracts did you land out of those people you reached out to?

Even with warm and hot audiences, it's key to stick with your funnel for 90 days minimum. Because (and this goes back to the educator analogy) when you switch your funnel, you've switched the assessment. You have mixed data that you can't compare over time. Just like we assess students the same way at the beginning and at the end of a unit or lesson plan, you need to stick with the same funnel so you can have a high-quality analysis.

GET YOUR FIRST (OR NEXT) CONTRACT

I want to offer you a few ways to find your first or next client. Remember, the goal of any (and all) of these strategies is to build, create, and maintain trust. That's why your TCF will move forward through any point of your funnel and sales process, and it is essential to them becoming a client.

Keeping that in mind, the first place to go is your own network. Don't discount the power of simply reaching out to people you know and talking about your business. Remember, these are folks who already know you, who want to support you, and would likely pay for your services—or refer you to someone who will—when they know your business exists.

I guarantee there are leads and money sitting in your contact list. When you're checking out who you know and who you are connected to, go beyond the obvious. While you can and should reach out to everyone in your network that fits your TCF profile, you can also reach out to people who are one degree removed from your target audience as well. These folks can facilitate introductions and make connections on your behalf once they know what you're doing and who you want to work with.

Let's talk through the steps of what I mean by working your network. The first step you can take is mapping out all the organizations and institutions you've interacted with during your career. Consider:

- who you've previously worked for;
- who you received training from;
- what schools, universities, etc., you attended; and
- what organizations you have led or been a member of.

This can end up being a lengthy list. When I did my own list, I went all the way back to my college internships with Limited Brands and Deloitte (when I thought I wanted to be a fashion merchandiser and was briefly also an accounting major), and even my high school.

I started my career in the Charlotte-Mecklenburg school district and also worked for Teach for America. I attended The Ohio State University (go Buckeyes) and got my doctorate at the Harvard Graduate School of Education. I'm also a proud, proud graduate of Columbus City Schools in Columbus, Ohio, where I grew up.

As for memberships, I am a member of The Collective, which is a national organization for alumni of color from Teach for America. I am an alumna of New Leaders, a principal-preparation program, and I completed the Leverage

Leadership Institute at Relay Graduate School of Education, where I was certified under the author of *Leverage Leadership*, Paul Bambrick-Santoyo.

That's a lot of places, spaces, and people—I'm sure you will have many too.

WERK YOUR NETWERK
JT'S EXAMPLE

PREVIOUS EMPLOYERS	TRAINING ORGS & ALMA MATERS	MEMBERSHIP AFFILIATIONS
·Limited Brands	·New Leaders	·Teach for America
·Deloitte	·Teach for America	·New Leaders
·Charlotte-Mecklenburg Schools	·The Ohio State University	·The Collective
·Teach for America	·Relay Graduate School of Education	·Leverage Leadership
	·Harvard Graduate School of Education	
	·Public Impact	
	·Columbus City Schools	

I want you to notice that I went all the way back to high school and college, because the objective of this particular exercise is to be as generative as possible. You could also include any affiliations or established networks, like alumni groups or sororities and fraternities. Your church or any religious organizations could be helpful. Include everywhere and everybody, because you never know who could one day give you a contract. For example, my doctorate program was a cohort model where I was one of 25 students. From that one program, I know three superintendents, a couple of educational leaders in state governments across the country, and a C-level officer at a nonprofit organization that funds a lot of educational nonprofits. All of those are potential leads for me either directly or indirectly.

In addition to looking at your own résumé and contact list, be sure to leverage platforms like LinkedIn where you have professional connections literally at your fingertips. When I was first building my consulting business, I would check my connections on LinkedIn for leads, because there were people there that I had forgotten about.

Once you have a list of people and organizations to reach out to, do a little research. For individuals, check out what they're up to now before sending an e-mail. When you want to leverage a connection to an organization, check out the work they're doing so that you know what might be available for you to help with. This strategy seems simple, but it's very effective. In the first few years of my own business, I was able to land several contracts by simply working my existing network.

Another strategy is to start by subcontracting. This is when another consultant outsources part of their work to someone else. Here's an example: Let's say Consultant A gets a big multi-six-figure contract but needs extra consultants to complete the work. Consultant A decides to hire Consultant B, Consultant C, and Consultant D to help, but because this is a single contract, Consultant A brings them on as subcontractors rather than W-2 employees. When Consultant A gets paid, they then pay out the others. In that scenario, if you are Consultant B (or C or D), you would actually be contracting with Consultant A and not the client.

To get work this way, reach out to fellow educational consultants that you know. I would recommend you reach out to them and schedule an informational interview to learn more about how they got started. In that conversation, you can ask how they found their first clients, what opportunities you can pass along to them so you can be a resource, and then share what your business is about and ask them to keep you in mind for any related opportunities. The intention would be to either receive referrals or be offered a contract as a subcontractor.

This is how I got my very first contract. At the time I was still a principal, and my boss, who I had a great relationship with, was a consultant on the side. I told her that I was interested in becoming a consultant and offered to take on jobs that she didn't have the capacity for. Within 30 days, she hit me up. Turns out she ended up having a conflict on the day a client had scheduled PD . . . and I was available. I didn't need a fancy funnel or even a website, because she knew me and knew I would deliver. That's the power of starting with your own network.

CHAPTER 8 REFLECTION QUESTIONS

1.   What mindset shift will be necessary for you to lean into selling in your business?

2.   How are you already generating traffic?

3.   If you have an existing business, what stages of the 7-FigurED Sales Funnel have you nailed, and which stages do you need to tighten up? What resources have you already created that you can repurpose into lead magnets?

ACTION STEPS

- Create your lead magnet.

- Set up your funnel.

- Identify a lead magnet for your audience. Identify 50 warm and hot leads to reach out to in the next 30 days.

- Track the conversion of your funnel weekly to make any small adjustments to improve your conversion.

7-FIGURE EDUCATOR RESOURCES

Visit **www.7febook.com/resources** to:

- Watch my Power Play episode "How I Landed My First $1,600 Consulting Contract"

  - Power Play episodes are short 8-to-15-minute mini lessons I have created to teach you a power play to implement in your business

- Watch my Power Play episode "Turning Conferences into Coins: A Step-by-Step Guide" that breaks down how to include conferences in your funnel to ensure you are leaving with leads and not empty-handed

- Grab my "Securing Your Next Client" module that will serve as next-layer support to help you identify your 50 leads

Grow

Brand Like a Bawse

*Objective: Build a marketing message
that attracts your target client*

Growing up, I heard a certain phrase all the time, and chances are you probably heard it too: *You have to work twice as hard.*

My mom, a baby boomer who grew up in rural Mississippi in the 1950s, knew that as a Black girl, I was likely to consistently be under a microscope while being simultaneously overlooked. Her way of preparing me for that harsh reality was to ensure that my success would be undeniable—because you can't be denied when you are two times better than everyone else. That meant I felt like I had to be two times better than every other applicant to get into the college I wanted to go to, two times better than any other first-year teacher to not be underestimated as the new kid on the block, two times better than every other applicant to that doctoral program at Harvard to be accepted, two times better than every other entrepreneur and every other education consultant to succeed.

You've probably heard something similar. For women, people of color, and anyone that is not a cisgender, heterosexual,

Christian white man whose first language is English—you have to be twice as good just to get by. Right? Right?

As it turns out? The answer is no.

But this untruth is one of those blessings in disguise. Because if you're anything like me and constantly heard this message growing up, it served you. And it served you well. I know that I've been successful partly *because* I thought I had to be twice as good as everyone else just to get by. And when I embodied that belief, *two times better, two times better, two times better*, I ended up—you guessed it—two times better.

Here's a prime example that still comes to mind every time I hear or write that phrase. Back when I was a Teach for America corps member, I was asked to speak on a panel at a fundraiser at a Professional Golfers' Association (PGA) tournament. The moment I was asked, I knew I would be one of the "only" in that room. And sure enough, when I showed up, I was the only one, and you couldn't miss me. There I was, on stage with the executive director of TFA for the region, the superintendent of my district, and the chairman of the golf tournament putting on the event—three white men. Though there were a few white ladies sipping drinks at the clubhouse, most of the people I could see were white men too.

But I was ready. I was going to be *two times better* than they expected. Not only had I written a great speech, but I had memorized it. I remember practicing in my bathroom mirror and reciting the words over and over again on my way to work. When I went to the microphone, I didn't need notes. I simply gave my speech, from memory, and then walked back to sit among my colleagues. After the event, the staff member who had selected me to speak said something like, "Wow, you memorized it!" But in my head, I was thinking, *I am not about to be one of the "only" in this room and be seen reading off a piece of paper.* Working twice as hard became my survival tactic in navigating a system that was not designed for me, a Black woman.

I'm sharing this example because I know you likely have a memory that's similar. Where you felt like you had to over-prepare, show up perfect, and be two times better. And while that approach has served us both well in the past, trust me, as an entrepreneur, this belief and approach will cause you to lose money, lose time, and undercut yourself.

My client Sharonda is a classic case study in how this coping mechanism has a serious expiration date. When I met her, Sharonda was in the process of starting a tutoring business as a side hustle. She had already been helping out casually after school with a few families, and saw an opportunity to make her business legit. But Sharonda had been struggling to take action.

Every weekend, she made a list of what she would accomplish. And every weekend, she got stuck when she didn't know where to start. There was so much to do. She needed a website, but, in order to do that, she had to get professional photos done, but to book that, she definitely needed to make appointments to get her hair braided, her nails done, oh, and obviously, find a new outfit, because the clothes she wore to teach just wouldn't do. And before doing any of that, Sharonda needed a logo and a brand name and a catchphrase, and wouldn't it be smart to get some branded clothing so that she could hand out T-shirts to the kids, and obviously those would need some kind of cute design, so she would have to find and hire a graphic designer, and . . . you see where I'm going.

Here's the catch: None of that was or is necessary—for you or for her. Sharonda could have legitimized her business and started making money within a single weekend. All she had to do was file her LLC, standardize her pricing, set up a way to take payments through a service like Stripe, Square, Pay-Pal, or Venmo, and ask her uncle who was an attorney to draft her a basic contract. Simple, right? But no. Sharonda felt like she had to be *two times better* and that she needed every single thing in place before she could approach the parents *she had already worked with* and ask to *continue* tutoring their kids.

Even though this chapter is literally about branding, I'm going to explain why you can get started exactly as you are, right now. Today. Without fancy photography, a beautiful website, or a logo of any kind. (Y'all—resist the logo! That 'ish is perfectionism and procrastination wrapped in Canva.) In fact, I'll show you the opposite—how and why starting with what you already know and who you already are generates money and momentum in your business.

Once we get past the window dressing of branding, we'll dig into what really matters: messaging. I'll walk you through the five components in my 7-FigurED Messaging framework and show you how a high school English lesson can help you tell a compelling story about your business that attracts even more TCFs. I'll show you how to showcase that messaging in every aspect of your marketing and sales, from social media and your e-mail list to proposals and one-on-one conversations. And I'll explain why all this will work when you put in consistent effort.

By the end of this chapter, you will know exactly how to build your brand from the bottom up, without getting stuck.

YOU DON'T NEED A LOGO

I've been an education consultant for a minute and in social groups with fellow entrepreneurs for longer. It's common for business owners to get stuck on the bells and whistles of branding—logos, company names, brand colors.

The flashy 'ish feels more pressing than what actually matters: Consistency. Visibility. Vulnerability. Showing up. Presenting yourself and your work to the world. Being seen.

But let's be real—vulnerability doesn't look the same for everyone. For people of color, especially Black women, being vulnerable can carry real risks. Speaking up or being visible in spaces not designed for us isn't always safe. That's why it's so important to recognize that safety can be found in creating your own system and your own rules.

That's what entrepreneurship makes possible. Vulnerability in business isn't about exposure for exposure's sake—it's about choosing how you show up, who you show up for, and on what terms. When you decide the rules, you decide the level of risk. And here's the truth: You don't need a logo to make you credible—you already are. Your expertise, your track record, and your results are what make you legitimate. The logo is just an accessory.

BUILDING YOUR BRAND

A brand isn't a logo or colors or even a company name. Instead, a brand is made up of the perception and *emotional* connection that a customer has with a company, product, service, or individual business owner. To build that, we need two components:

1. Marketing messaging
2. Ways to share that messaging with your different audiences (cold, warm, hot)

An intentional brand that comes to mind for me is Savage X Fenty. Yes, Rihanna is the face of the company. But when you zoom out and look at the brand as a whole—the models in their runway shows, the ads they run, the way they market— there is a clear message being sent. Fenty has a clear marketing message of inclusivity, sex positivity (especially for women), and celebrating all bodies. Savage X Fenty intentionally leverages partnerships with celebrities and micro-influencers of all different identities, which purposely celebrates diversity and individuality while also expanding their reach.

Here's another example. Ben & Jerry's. Sure, they sell ice cream, but the brand's marketing is heavily based on the company's activism, specifically in the areas of social and economic justice, human rights, and the environment. Ben & Jerry's has clearly made an effort to put their activism at the front, even though they sell what seems like an unrelated product. Savage X Fenty's marketing showcases inclusivity and diversity and shows the company's commitment to those values (and to making those values sexy). I share these two companies specifically because I want you to notice how their branding and marketing messages are communicated. The impact of the messaging is clear and creates a response in the minds of customers, who then choose to buy (or not) based on this branding.

Branding matters to your whole audience but is an absolute nonnegotiable when it comes to your cold audience. Cold audiences require marketing and branding because that is how we begin to build a relationship with people who don't know us (yet). Like we discussed in Chapter 8, people can't become loyal without first becoming aware of who you are and what you're about. You need to build an intentional strategy around how to position yourself in your market so that your cold audience becomes aware of you and wants to learn more.

This is where the work you've done so far really starts to come together into a marketing and branding strategy. You will use the market research and TCF profile you created in Chapter 6 to create your marketing message and the funnel you created in Chapter 8 to test with cold audiences for at least the next 90 days through the three levers I'm going to share.

Let me remind you: We won't be discussing logos in this chapter, because they are accessories. So you can go ahead and close your Canva app, boo.

7-FIGURED BRAND MESSAGING

Before you dive into this particular framework, I'm gonna need you to grab your TCF profile and the notes you took on the market research you did after reading Chapter 6. Those are your resource materials. There are five components within this framework, and I want you to approach each of them with a generative, expansive mindset. For each of the five components, I want you to create a list of possibilities. The bigger your list, the better, because the more choices you have, the clearer you'll get. And clarity is key to being able to hit on all five components in the messaging you create.

1. Pain Points

These are the symptoms of the problem that your client is experiencing, not necessarily the problem itself. For example, if the problem you're solving is helping new teachers master classroom management, some of the symptoms might be that they end the day exhausted and their kids aren't learning despite their best efforts. Another symptom might be that they stay up late every night planning but know their lesson plan isn't as effective as it could be. Or maybe it takes them 15 minutes every day to get back into the classroom from lunch because all the kids are talking and they lose instructional time. Those are all symptoms of the problems, which means those are great pain points.

This is why I asked you to grab all the work from Chapter 6, because this is where your market research becomes essential. For your pain points to resonate, you need to have very clear language and examples in your TCF's own words.

Let me give you an example from my own business. When you check out my social media, you might hear me say that you're overworked and underpaid as an educator. Because that's a pain point my target audience has told me that y'all are experiencing. And the fact that I can speak to it helps to build trust, because it's clear I get what educators are going through.

If you are having trouble finding your TCF's pain points, then you may need to go back to Chapter 6 and redo the homework. It's likely that you don't have enough market research. There's no shame in having to schedule a few more informational interviews; this part of the work is important to get right.

2. Desires

What are your TCF's deepest desires? What do they day-dream about? What do they wish were true about their careers or their lives or the world? At the end of the day, underneath everything, what do they want?

In my experience, your TCF either wants to make something, save something, protect something, improve something, reduce something, or increase something. It's your job to figure out what that is. What's the *desire* behind the solution you provide? Does your TCF wanna make more money? Save time? Improve their community? Reduce their anxiety?

Increase their confidence? Those are broad examples, because I want you to think expansively. Don't just figure out one desire and be done; be generative. Use your pain points as a starting place. If those pain points were resolved, what would your TCF get? How would they feel?

Another quick example from my business. My target client wants to make a bigger impact while also making more money. That's only one desire, and it's hella simple, but it is the exact thing my target client (and likely you too) has in mind, so it works.

3. Transformation

This is the literal change that clients will experience as a result of working with you. A "how it started"-versus-"how it's going" type of energy. Articulating the transformation from before to after is crucial, because some of your clients know they have an issue but don't know what a solution looks and feels like. When your TCF is so steeped in the problem, they might not be able see a way out or know what it would feel like to no longer have the problem. That gives you an opportunity to explain and show how working with you provides a solution they might not even know existed.

The transformation that I use in my own messaging is "going from overworked and underpaid to a life of financial ease while having double the impact, double the income, and working half the time." Powerful.

4. Values

It may not feel like you have a company yet, but you do have a company. As a business owner, your values are going to be the basis for the decisions and moves you make. It's time to draft the core values you want to embody within your own business, because this is a key part of your messaging. It will also inform who you hire and how you'll grow. So this piece is as much for you as it is for your TCF. Often these values will reflect your own personal values.

I created six core values for my company: self-care is preservation; we build wealth responsibly; we value authenticity; joy is an act of resistance; results matter; and we wave our receipts with no shame. Those values are why you'll never see me on the Internet claiming to be humble. That's because, to me, sharing my authentic wins is not arrogant; it's stating facts.

5. Testimonials

Your cold audience (and perhaps even warm/hot folks) will want to hear from your previous clients. That's why it is important to get in the habit of collecting testimonials. Even if you haven't had a paid client (yet), you could still collect testimonials from people that you've worked with. Case in point: When I first launched my consulting business, the very first testimonial I got was from my assistant principal. I told her I was launching my business to coach other school leaders and asked for her to share a little bit about what it was like working with me.

Testimonials help us create our marketing messaging, because when you have a testimonial, you have both social proof and the exact words of your client. Before you go on any further, do a testimonial audit. Make sure that you have, or have asked for, a testimonial from every client you've worked with. If you're early in the process of building your business and haven't worked with many clients yet, tap into your network. Reach out to your colleagues, former supervisors, parents, and so on. Ask for testimonials from folks who fit your TCF profile or are connected to folks who fit.

MINING FOR MESSAGING

In addition to doing market research, I want you to intentionally go looking for your TCF online. You're going to lurk, but not in a creepy way. Your goal is to better understand who you're trying to serve. You are going to get into the practice of reading, hearing, and experiencing the words of your target client when they talk about the problem that your business solves.

Social media is helpful for this. Facebook groups are great, because people join looking for solutions from their peers. When you join those groups, be sure to read the posts to see what people are talking about. Look for how your TCF expresses their pain points, their desires, the transformation they are seeking, and maybe even their values. Another place to look is YouTube. You can search for the most frequently asked questions about the problem you solve and check out the comment sections. Google and Reddit can also be great resources for finding your TCF's exact words in expressing their frustrations and challenges. Don't sleep on your own audience and network either. You can directly ask your audience what their biggest pain point is around the problem your business solves. You could do that through your e-mail list or on social media, through a formal survey, or in DM conversations.

When you start to see the same language repeated by different people that meet your TCF profile . . . copy and paste that into your own marketing messaging. It might feel odd to use words that aren't your own, but research has shown that leveraging the exact phrases that your ideal customers use makes your messaging far more effective. Check it out: In 2023, researchers published a study in the academic journal *Psychology and Marketing* that looked at thousands of customer reviews from airports around the world. What they found is that when airports used the exact words of their customers' pain points in marketing, customers found the communication more relevant and emotionally resonant. As a result, customers demonstrated more brand loyalty, engagement, and satisfaction.

I've seen this be successful in my own business. I didn't come up with the phrase "overworked and underpaid" to describe my TCF's pain point. That didn't come from me; it came from a Facebook group where my TCFs shared how many hours they worked and how underpaid they felt. I simply took that language and incorporated it into my marketing message. Turns out that study was right. When I started using my TCF's exact words, the response I got was stronger, because my message resonated more.

By describing exactly what your TCF is thinking, feeling, and quite literally *saying* online, you can create more emotional resonance, which makes them more likely to engage and ultimately, to buy.

CRAFTING YOUR MARKETING MESSAGE

When I'm teaching about content, I often share examples of what not to do as a sort of no-shame show-and-tell. Here is one of my favorite nonexamples: *Our PD series includes four half-day sessions aligned to our leadership framework.*

Do you see a pain point in this message? How about a desire? Any transformation? Values? There's clearly not a testimonial . . . but seriously. If you are thinking of times when you shared a marketing message like this and are cringing inside, that's okay. I'm about to teach you what you need to know. The biggest mistake in the marketing message I just shared is that it lacks emotion and connection.

Research from Gallup shows only 30 percent of our purchase-making decisions are based on rational factors, while 70 percent are based on emotion. There's even a study out of Harvard saying that 95 percent of this decision-making is done in the subconscious mind. To ethically use that information to your advantage, your marketing message needs to do two things: sell the dream while also acknowledging the nightmare. To do that effectively, we get to use a tool that most educators know how to use well. Storytelling. Specifically, the elements of a plot. ELA teachers, it's time to give you your shine!

To tell a good story, you need five parts: the exposition, rising action, climax, following action, and resolution. We're going to use this framework but translate it to marketing.

Exposition → Hook (attention grabber or distinct point of view)

Rising Action → Pain (how your TCF experiences the pain points)

Climax → Partnership (how y'all can work together to solve the problem)

Falling Action → Transformation (what will happen when your TCF works with you)

Resolution → Testimony (previous results and testimonials from past clients)

Let me walk you through an example using that same PD series I mentioned at the beginning of this section. The offer is a four-part series of half-day PDs that helps school leaders manage their time more effectively. So, a marketing message that serves as a hook, or the distinct POV, could be something like *Even if you worked 24 hours in a day, you wouldn't have enough time to run your building. That's because the issue isn't needing more time, it's your lack of trust and delegation.*

The point of the hook is to literally hook your TCF and keep them reading.

Next, talk about the pain. Remember, you want to find and use your TCF's exact words at this part of the message. Here's an example: *You are the first one in the building and the last one to leave, but your to-do list doesn't feel any shorter.*

Once you have created emotional connection and resonance, you can describe the partnership, which is how you and your offers can help. Be sure to describe the service in the following cadence:

- Acknowledge the *pain point.*

- Name the service *feature* that addresses the pain point.

- Share the *benefit* of the specific feature, meaning what your client gains because of it.

Your partnership message could be something like . . .

Your calendar feels like a monster that can't be slayed on its own (pain point). *Our PD series includes a seat for your admin assistant or staff member that handles your calendar* (feature). *The job of a school leader is BIG. You don't have time to review every calendar request that comes your way. We know school leaders need someone to block and tackle the endless requests for their time, and having your admin by your side during this training will ensure you have the help you need to slay the day and your calendar* (benefit).

I want you to specifically notice the emotion. You could just name the feature ("bring your admin" or "you get a plus-one"), but that would not have the same resonance as sharing the benefit as well.

Next, you should talk about the transformation, which is how your TCF will experience their life or work differently as a result of working with you. For instance: *You're gonna go from overwhelmed and stressed about your to-do list to building trust through strategic delegation.*

And last, a testimonial:

"When I found Dr. EJT, I felt like I was getting nothing done even though I was at school for 10 to 12 hours every day. Thanks to our work together in just a few half-day sessions, I was able to get organized and delegate to my team effectively and strategically. Thanks to Dr. EJT, I leave school every day at 4 P.M. feeling like I've conquered the world. I turn my work phone off with no guilt as soon as I step in the house and am finally able to be present with my family."

Remember, your marketing messages are content that can be used multiple times on different platforms and for different purposes. A common misconception is that you can't repeat the same message—essentially if you say it once, you can't say it again. But that's simply not true, especially online. Personally, I can barely remember what I posted yesterday, much less what anyone else has said.

Just like you might have had to teach the same lesson three different ways in the classroom, you might need to express the same marketing message on three different platforms or over a series of posts for people to "get" what you're saying. It's okay to send an e-mail to your e-mail list in the morning and then use content from that e-mail as the caption for a social media post later on in the day. Don't be afraid to recycle your content, especially the messages that you see perform well. Normalize for yourself that people need to see your message multiple times and that, just like our students, seeing it multiple times helps with internalization and understanding. Not to mention that you're getting new eyes on your content every day! Those folks shouldn't miss out on learning just because they didn't know you existed yesterday.

MARKETING TOUCHPOINTS

Remember, the first interaction your client has with you and your brand isn't onboarding. Instead, it's through your marketing, specifically at the traffic-generation or awareness stage. You need to define what that interaction feels and looks like from the perspective of your client and think about that perspective as they move from awareness to conversion. According to research, the average customer requires an average of eight touchpoints during the marketing and sales process to convert from someone who doesn't know you at all to becoming a client.

That said, I always encourage more touchpoints, because your customers may require a higher level of trust to make a buying decision. Your TCF may want to feel like they know you better or have a deeper relationship before they pull out their credit card. That's especially true when money feels tight, like when the broader economy is contracting. (Even a trust recession, where the economy is doing okay but people *feel* financially stressed, creates more skepticism and can affect your ability to convert folks.) So, instead of 6 to 8 touchpoints in your marketing, you may need 12 touchpoints, maybe even up to 16, to get from awareness to conversion.

I want to be really clear that touchpoints aren't always selling. A post on social media or a reel could be a touchpoint. Every e-mail in a welcome sequence is a touchpoint. A free resource or opt-in could be a touchpoint. A phone call or sales conversation is a touchpoint; a text message is a touchpoint. There are lots of different ways to design your touchpoints, but it's important to be thoughtful and intentional that each one creates value for your TCF.

Once you know what your touchpoints will be, you can systematize and automate your marketing. That takes your (manual) hands off the wheel and frees you up to do other things, including working with paid clients.

Do a content audit

Wondering how you are going to create 12 to 16 touchpoints? If you've been in business for a minute, you've probably already done it. I challenge you to conduct a content audit. When I say "content," I mean social media posts, lives, shorts, and reels. I mean client testimonials. I mean blog posts. I mean any type of short-form or long-form video content. I mean any type of templates, resources, articles, anything you've written. If you've been a guest on a podcast, that's another piece of content.

What most people realize when they go through this activity are two things: First, you've been sitting on a gold mine of content. And, second, that you haven't been using or leveraging most of it within your business. But now you can by using that content in your marketing, or incorporating it into other touchpoints, like client-renewal conversations or following up on sales conversations like discovery and consultation calls.

TWO LEVERS TO SHOWCASE YOUR BRANDING

Now that you know how to put together effective marketing messages *and* create the touchpoints necessary to convert your TCF, you get to choose *how* and *where* you're gonna say all that. Though I'm about to offer two different levers, the idea isn't that you'll master both tomorrow. Instead, I want you to pick an entry point and focus on being consistent with posting or sharing your marketing message. Once you have mastered executing your marketing message really well and are able to start measuring its efficacy, you can add another lever.

1. E-Mail List

I don't have many regrets in life, but I will admit that I waited too long to build an e-mail list. This is the first branding lever that I want you to use. An e-mail list is the best way to directly reach your hot and warm audiences—and an easy way to build and nurture your relationships with your leads.

Think of your e-mail list as your own little corner of the Internet where people are there to learn more about you and from you. An e-mail list builds trust through storytelling and sharing your expertise. To begin, I recommend using an e-mail software like Kit, because you will quickly outgrow any DIY solution like a spreadsheet. There are lots of ways to leverage your list, and I've provided the best and current ways in the online resources for this book.

E-mail can be a lucrative branding lever because the average conversion rate of e-mail marketing is 1 to 2 percent. What that means is when you communicate with your e-mail list consistently—sending an e-mail at least once a week— you can expect that 1 to 2 percent of your total audience on any given campaign will convert to a purchase. So, if you have an e-mail list of 100 people, you can convert 1 person. If you have an e-mail list of 1,000 people, you could convert 10 people. This is why starting as early as possible with your e-mail list is so important, because the earlier you can start collecting e-mails, the earlier you can start gaining subscribers. Once you get to ~100,000 or so subscribers, your 1 percent conversion is now 1,000 people—who become clients.

> ## THE ONE-PAGE WEBSITE
>
> If you want to have a page where people can read your bio, see a few testimonials, and contact you, consider a landing page. This is a single-page website that you can build on your own quickly and is a great alternative to a full-blown website. For my current recommendations, check out the online resources for this book.

2. Social Media

The second lever is social media. Whether you decide to prioritize Facebook, Instagram, LinkedIn, TikTok, YouTube, or any new platform that has become popular by the time you're reading this, I encourage you to pick a single platform to go hard on. Partly because I want you to succeed at being consistent and partly because each platform operates differently. Here are three considerations when deciding which platform to start with:

1. Where your target audience is most likely to show up

As of 2025:

- Facebook is mostly used by people over 30, with 78 percent of people between 30 and 49 using the service and 70 percent of people aged 50 to 64.

- Instagram is mostly used by people under 50, with the biggest demographics being people between 18 and 29 (76 percent) and 30 to 49 (66 percent).

- LinkedIn users are solidly between 25 to 55, with over 68 percent of users in that age range.

- TikTok is dominated by people under 35, with 69 percent of people in their 20s using the app.

- YouTube is used by nearly all age groups, with roughly 80 to 90 percent of adults under 65 using the platform.

2. The type of content the platform is built for

LinkedIn is great for written content, YouTube is best for mid- and long-form content. TikTok is great for short-form content.

3. What platforms you already have traction on

For example, when I first started my business, I went hard on Facebook on my personal account because I already had about 8,000 followers there. Instead of building new attention, I leveraged the attention I already had.

WHAT DO I POST?

There are three types of posts that work well on social media:

Visibility. These posts let people know that you and your business exist. This could be pictures of you presenting at a conference. Or, if your target client desires flexibility of their time and schedule, a photo of you at the beach where you talk about that flexibility in the caption.

Expertise. The objective here is to position yourself and your brand as an expert in your given field. This is where you might share pieces of your framework or resources, thoughts, and information related to the problem that your business solves.

Offer. These are direct posts that are telling people about your offer. To do this, you could use testimonials of clients that share their experience of what it's like to work with you. You could say something like, "I have an upcoming workshop, and here's why you need to attend."

WHY YOUR BRANDING AND MARKETING WILL WORK . . . WHEN YOU WORK IT

Using marketing to build your brand is like pushing a flywheel. At first, a flywheel takes a lot of momentum and effort to get going. Back in the day, these large metal disks weighed thousands of pounds. But once you get it going, the flywheel moves faster and faster until you don't need to put in as much effort to get the same results. Each turn of the flywheel builds upon work that you did earlier to create momentum.

This is called the flywheel effect, and it was first described in the best-selling book *Good to Great* by business expert and author Jim Collins. He argued that in any successful enterprise, there isn't a single action or breakthrough moment. Instead, it's the *accumulation* of effort in a consistent direction that matters. Your goal is to put in that initial effort and get your own flywheel going. I recognize that what I've outlined in this chapter is a lot of work. But that work is necessary for you to start pushing the flywheel of your business forward. You may see small results at first. Maybe only one person signs up for your e-mail list, or you gain only 10 social media followers a week. That's okay. It's normal. But what will happen when you stay consistent is that eventually, your flywheel will begin to turn faster and faster with the same amount of effort from you. That 1 e-mail subscriber will turn into 10. Those 10 social media followers will become 100, and so on.

When you use what you've learned in this chapter and combine it with flexing your funnel, you will gain momentum. Soon you'll be able to gain followers who will become customers, who will provide you with more testimonials and referrals, gaining you more followers who will become e-mail subscribers, who will become customers who will provide you with more testimonials . . . and soon that flywheel of yours is flying all on its own.

Meaning that instead of feeling like you have to work twice as hard or do twice as much to get what you deserve, you can start where you are now, knowing that you'll end up right where you want to be.

CHAPTER 9 REFLECTION QUESTIONS

1. What visibility mindsets will you need to manage as you fully lean into branding in your business?

2. Take a moment and think about the brands that resonate with you. What do those brands have in common? Look out for, observe, and notice the successful marketing messages you see out in the world (and online) for examples of what you can do for your own business.

3. Aside from your e-mail list, what is ONE branding lever that you will start with as a marketing priority in your business?

4. What are the daily and weekly actions you can take to build your flywheel momentum?

ACTION STEPS

Brainstorm the 7-FigurED Brand Messaging components based on your TCF's:

- Pain points
- Desires
- Transformation
- Values
- Testimonials

Mine for messaging from your TCF on social media. Craft marketing messages that include:

- Hook
- Pain
- Partnership
- Transformation
- Testimony

Choose one branding lever and share your marketing message(s).

7-FIGURE EDUCATOR RESOURCES

Visit www.7febook.com/resources to:

- Read about the Flywheel Effect from Jim Collins
- Access my content-audit worksheet and tutorial video

- Watch Episode 53: "Content That Converts: Social Media Strategies 7-Figure Entrepreneurs Use with Kasey Brown" of the *7-Figure Educator* podcast, where I sit down with a social media expert and discuss best practices for social media content

- Watch Episode 50: "Proven Storytelling Strategies to Attract Ideal Clients & Grow Your Business with Andy Henriquez" of the *7-Figure Educator* podcast, where I have a conversation with a storytelling expert to unpack the elements of effective storytelling

Hire Your Right Hand

Objective: Create systems and SOPs so you can hire a team

If you're like the majority of my clients when they first start working with me, you do everything in your business yourself. Every e-mail is sent by you from your inbox. Every social media post involves you opening up your app. Every invoice is sent by your hands. Most of the educators I work with start their business off as me, myself, and I. And this isn't just personal preference; it's connected to a larger story. According to the Brookings Institution, 96 percent of Black-owned businesses are sole proprietorships. That number doesn't just reflect hustle; it also reflects history. The way white-supremacy culture has elevated individualism over collectivism shapes how we've been taught to build. Add that cultural pressure to the very real fear of being responsible for someone else's paycheck as an employer, and it makes sense why so many of us hesitate to hire. What I want you to recognize, though, is that as a sole proprietor, you will eventually hit a limit on how much revenue, profit, and wealth you can generate. In fact, research shows that only 17 percent of solo businesses reach $100,000 or more in annual revenue. And only a tiny fraction—0.02 percent to be exact—earn more than a million dollars.

Contrast that with Black-owned businesses with employees, where 10 to 15 percent earn over a million dollars in revenue annually and 60 to 70 percent earn six figures. To grow, you will need to hire. And to hire, you'll need to grow, specifically by putting systems and infrastructure in place so that you can train and delegate effectively.

That's what this chapter is about. I'll teach you why it is inherently risky to build a business that's dependent solely on you. Systems might not seem flashy, but I'm going to teach you why standard operating procedures (SOPs) are the foundation to growing your business and your personal wealth. I'll explain why standardizing your operations positions your business to grow to seven figures (and beyond). I'll offer an SOP template along with the three actions that you need to systematize.

From there, I'll show you how to hire. I'll explain who your first hire needs to be and how to intentionally build your team, and offer an exercise to help you understand exactly what you need help with. After that I'll walk you through the process I have successfully used to hire both as a principal and as a seven-figure business owner. We'll talk about how to classify team members as either contractors or employees, design your org chart, and incorporate payroll into your business finances while retaining profit.

By the end of this chapter, you will know exactly what you need to do to standardize, systematize, and scale your business.

YOUR BUSINESS ISN'T YOUR BABY

Pull your toes in, because I'm gonna step on 'em.

If you can't take six months off from your business without everything falling apart, you're not an entrepreneur. Yet.

That's because you may have fallen into one of the easiest traps there is in business: having everything depend on you. I first learned about this stumbling block at the London School of Business, where I participated in an educational program for entrepreneurs. The conversation among the program's seven-, eight-, and nine-figure entrepreneurs wasn't about improving the internal workings of their businesses. Instead, these entrepreneurs were focused on understanding the value of their businesses to potential investors and buyers, with the intention of one day not working in their business at all. I spoke with one entrepreneur from California who worked only 10 hours a week—meeting with the leadership team he had hired to replace him.

What I learned in those conversations was really simple. Most of us start businesses as a way to get free. But along the way, we build companies that are dependent on us. Our expertise. Our way of doing things. Our leadership. Our decision-making. And with a lot of online brands, our personality or even our image. But that comes with a lot of cost— and less freedom.

According to *Forbes*, building a business that is dependent on you:

- constrains growth because you become the bottleneck for all decisions;

- requires overworking from the founder (you), which can lead to feeling overwhelmed and burned out, and can affect your overall health; and

- undermines the financial value of your business, making it difficult to sell.

You may not plan to ever sell your business, and that's fine. However, understanding how the people who invest in and acquire businesses value those businesses can help us understand how to future-proof our own. Future-proofing includes making a shift from thinking like a small business owner and CEO to the mindset of a founder and investor. People who buy and sell businesses are interested in buying ownership, and as we talked about in Chapter 2, ownership is about intellectual property and systems.

When I teach about systems and why they are important, I often bring up the story of *The Three Little Pigs*. One little pig built a house made out of straw, one built a house made out of sticks, and one built a house made out of bricks. And then along came a big, bad wolf to blow their houses down. The Big Bad Wolf was able to blow down the house of straw; it was able to blow down the house of sticks. But it was not able to blow down the house of bricks. The lesson in this story is that **how you build matters.**

When there are no systems in a business, the owner has built a house of straw. The business is dependent entirely on the owner's presence and effort. When the owner gets sick, when the owner takes a vacation, when life starts life-ing, the business will be negatively impacted and may even fail. When your house is built of straw, *key person risk* is the Big Bad Wolf that can blow your whole house down.

When a business has systems, but those systems are broken or incomplete or go unused, that business is built of sticks. This is still a risky position because the business is likely still dependent on the owner to operate.

But when a business owner takes the time to create a system for everything they do, systems that can be duplicated by anyone—they have built a house of bricks that will remain standing when wolves try to blow the damn house down. There's no key person risk, because the systems—not individual people—allow the business to run. When your business becomes a house of bricks, you can take time off, knowing that your business will run just fine without you. This is also when you can move from CEO to founder and focus on alignment instead of day-to-day operations.

Forget that straw and them sticks—we are building a sturdy house of bricks.

CREATING SYSTEMS

The time to build systems in your business is when you have clarity around your offers, efficacy in your marketing message, and consistent monthly revenue. You'll also know that it's time to standardize your operations when your business starts to break. For example, maybe you onboard every client you work with individually, and while that may have been fine for a small number of clients, after a certain number of them, onboarding might not happen when or how it needs to.

Implementing systems and standard operating procedures into your business means no longer doing everything yourself. That may feel scary, because educators often believe that nobody else can teach the way we can—so we *have* to do everything ourselves. But what I want you to recognize is that your gifts can become clouded by a lack of systems. The experience that your client has is not exclusive to the quality of the service you offer. Instead, it's tied to their holistic experience. The people you work with are far less likely to remember how great your delivery of the services were if you don't respond to e-mails.

What I see in communities of education consultants and entrepreneurs isn't a lack of knowledge or passion. Most people know their 'ish, offer great services, and are doing the best they can on their own. But the lack of systems within their business affects their ability to create and deliver the high-quality client experience that unlocks more revenue and growth.

Now that you understand why to implement systems in your business (and why that might feel scary), I will lead you through the how.

Systems are built on SOPs

Creating SOPs helps to define each step of a process for yourself and your team and ensures consistency in everything you do. As educators, we are all too familiar with SOPs. Every educator I know knows what's supposed to happen when you hear someone on the intercom say "lockdown." Everybody knows you close your classroom door, pull the shades on your windows, turn off the lights, gather your students in the corner farthest away from the door, and stay silent. No matter what school you're in, how old the kids in your class are, what state you lead or teach in. You know what to do for a lockdown.

The purpose of any SOP is to define the steps of a system so that anyone following those steps will deliver the same outcome every time. Part of your work as a small business owner is to create your own SOPs. This will allow you to be able to hire, train, and delegate to team members effectively.

Creating SOPs before you have a team in place will help you stay ready so you don't have to get ready. A mistake that many entrepreneurs make is expecting new hires to know how you want things done. But without SOPs, you're asking them to read your mind. By outlining some or most of your SOPs before you hire, you give yourself an advantage by being able to train future team members quickly and effectively.

As you continue to grow your business, and build out your team, every department will have SOPs. The sales department will have SOPs that document your sales process: how you lead sales calls, how you capture lead notes, how you nurture leads, etc. The operations department will have SOPs that document the backend of your business: your customer refund policy, procedures for the client inbox, steps to change client information on file, etc. The marketing department will have SOPs to outline your content creation process, how you upload your podcast to YouTube, how to run a marketing campaign debrief meeting, etc. You following me here? Everything in your business should be documented.

Think of it this way: If someone was out sick, anyone should be able to step in and fulfill their duties—and SOPs are their "sub binder."

There are endless examples of potential SOPs, but I want you to start with the heart of your business, the client experience. Specifically, your first SOPs should be for:

- client onboarding

- client delivery

- client offboarding

Drafting SOPs

Let's start with how you title your SOPs. File names can seem inconsequential, but imagine having a seven-figure business with literally hundreds of SOPs. 'Ish will get messy real quick if you don't use a naming convention to organize yourself. Here's an example of how to use a naming convention to title an SOP:

SOP_OP_001_Client Onboarding

All SOPs should start with *SOP* in the naming conventions. Next is the department. *OP* is short for "operations." You might use *MK* for "marketing" and *SL* for "sales." Next is the SOP number. No fancy logic to it other than number the SOPs as they are created, so in this example, *001* means this was the first SOP created in the operations department. Last, *Client Onboarding* is the brief title of what the SOP is about.

Now that I have set you up for success organizing your SOPs (you can thank me later!), let's dive into the actual content of the SOP. It's important to remember that SOPs exist so that you and your team can complete tasks efficiently. An SOP is ineffective if folks get lost in the sauce. You want to provide enough detail so that the average person can follow along, but not so much that people get confused. The aim is simple, one- or two-sentence instructions. I recommend every SOP you create include:

- Description
- Purpose
- Resources
- Video instructions
- Step-by-step written instructions
- Tips & traps

Let's walk through each section, and I'll provide an example for every item. The first section of your SOP is a **description**. This section explains the purpose of the SOP and the specific task, process, or activity it covers. Think of it as the "what and why" of the procedure: what the SOP is for and why it matters for the business. A clear description sets the context so that anyone reading the SOP knows exactly when and why to use it.

Here's an example:

This SOP outlines the process for onboarding new clients into our services. It ensures every client has a smooth, consistent, and welcoming experience from the moment they sign their contract through their first seven days of working with us. The onboarding process includes communication touchpoints, account setup, and initial orientation steps that set the tone for a successful client relationship.

The second section of your SOP is **purpose**. This section defines why the SOP matters and the results it's meant to deliver. It links the step-by-step task to the larger goals of the business, whether that's creating consistency, improving efficiency, or elevating the client experience. A clear purpose ensures your team understands not just what to do, but the impact of doing it well.

Your purpose section could look like this:

> The purpose of this SOP is to ensure every new client has a consistent, professional, and welcoming onboarding experience. This process is designed to build trust from day one, set clear expectations, and equip clients with the tools and information they need to fully engage with our services. By standardizing onboarding, we create efficiency for the team while also laying the foundation for a long-term, successful client relationship.

The **resource** section lists all the tools, systems, templates, or documents required to complete the process. Think of it as a checklist of everything someone would need before they start so the procedure can be carried out smoothly without delays.

Here's a sample of what a resource section might look like:

RESOURCES

- contract template (stored in Google Drive → client docs folder)

- e-signature software (e.g., Docusign or HelloSign)

- welcome e-mail template (stored in the e-mail marketing platform or SOP folder)

- CRM or client database access (to update client information once onboarding is complete)

- scheduling tool (e.g., Calendly link for the 30-minute kickoff call)

Video instructions are a great way to document your processes in real time and construct an SOP from how you complete the task today. This is simple to create. Using software like Loom or Zoom, you just record yourself completing the task and talking through all the steps as you go.

Step-by-step written instructions are exactly what that sounds like. Be sure to keep this section clear, concise, and to the point. You can include screenshots in this section as well.

Here is a very basic example:

STEP-BY-STEP INSTRUCTIONS

Send Contract

- Open the contract template, personalize client details, and send via e-signature tool.

- Once signed, download the PDF. Save it to the Client Folder.

Send Welcome E-mail

- Send within 24 business hours of receipt of signed contract.

- Use the Welcome E-mail template; personalize name, program, and start date.

- Include link to schedule 30-Minute Kickoff Call.

- When booked, add the calendar invite (include Zoom/agenda), and confirm with the client.

Prep & Handoff

- Create the kickoff agenda doc.

- Schedule a reminder to be sent 24 hours prior to the kickoff call.

Last, you may want to also include **tips and traps**. These are certain parts of the task that folks need to pay close attention to, shortcuts, common issues, or best practices. Here's an example:

TIPS & TRAPS

Tips

- Use templates (contract + welcome e-mail) to save time and keep messaging consistent.

- Double-check that the client's name, program details, and start date are correct before sending any documents.

Traps

- Delaying the welcome e-mail beyond 24 business hours of a signed contract. Waiting too long can make new clients feel forgotten.

- Forgetting to save the signed contract in the client folder. This creates chaos when you need it later.

Be sure to use the same format every time, and mark when the SOP was last updated in the document. Over time, these will become fail-proof systems in your business. I have included a sample SOP in the online resources for this chapter to give you a more detailed example.

Create your own operations hub

As you create SOPs for every process in your business, set up an "operations hub" where the link to every SOP lives. This creates a library for the future and allows for quick reference when you bring on new team members or need to check that you're doing things as intended and designed. Be sure to review all the SOPs in your Operations Hub regularly (at least every quarter) to ensure that everything is up to date.

HIRING YOUR RIGHT HAND

Obama had Biden, Beyoncé had Kelly, Jordan had Pippen, and every education consultant who has a seven-figure business has a #2 on their team, aka a "right hand." When it's time to hire your right hand, approach the process with strategy and intention. This role is complex, underrated, and highly valuable, which means it deserves more than a rushed decision made out of desperation when you're overwhelmed. The right hire sets the foundation for sustainable scaling, while the wrong hire can cost you time, money, and momentum.

I know this because the first time I hired a virtual assistant, I made all the mistakes. I was in my doctoral program at Harvard, classes were starting, and my education consulting business was in growth mode. I needed help, like, yesterday. I threw up a job posting online and hired the first person who showed interest. What I realized later was that I would never have been that casual or rushed as a principal. The students and teachers I led were too important—and my business should have been too. In the end, that first virtual assistant lasted only a few months, because it was clear that we were not a good fit. The next time I was more intentional about my hiring process and found someone so amazing that, five years later, they're still on my team.

How to Figure Out Who You Need

Before we get into the hiring process, you need to you guessed it—collect data.

The best way to figure out the specific support you need is to conduct a time study. You want to see how you're actually spending your time, so you can determine what tasks you want to keep on your plate and what you'd like to delegate.

So, what is a time study?

It's a process that allows you to track your time, your tasks, and to what extent you are spending your time on revenue-generating activity. Ideally you will track this data for two weeks. The goal is to get a thorough picture, which you're not gonna get if you decide to take a shortcut and study yourself for only a day or two. That's why we're committing to two full weeks of tracking what you're doing every 15 minutes. Yes, it sounds tedious, but I get excited when I think about all the juicy data you're going to get from approaching your work and business this way. I hope you do too.

Every 15 minutes, you're gonna be tracking three things:

1. the tasks you are doing
2. whether or not those tasks are revenue-generating activity
3. whether or not the task brings you joy

Keep in mind, this is not a journal entry or a deep dive. Writing these three details every 15 minutes should take you only a minute or two. For example, entries in a time study look like this:

TIME	TASK	REVENUE GENERATING?	BRINGS YOU JOY?

TIME	TASK	REVENUE GENERATING?	BRINGS YOU JOY?
9:45 A.M.	Answered e-mails	No	No
10:00 A.M.	Wrote a proposal	Yes	Yes

See how simple this is? I want to give you some examples of revenue-generating tasks, because this can feel fuzzy to folks. Anything that leads to making you money is a revenue-generating task. Whether you're generating traffic, leads, or qualifying clients, those are all revenue-generating activities. Money-generating activities include every part of the sales process.

A great example of a revenue-generating task is a sales or discovery call, where you're directly talking to a client about the next step toward actually engaging in your services.

Another revenue-generating task might be drafting or sending a proposal or hosting a workshop.

Tasks that aren't revenue generating are less tied to sales and generating money. For example, editing your website is not revenue generating. Neither is creating a graphic in Canva. Editing a podcast episode doesn't make you any money. Responding to e-mails isn't revenue generating unless you are qualifying a lead to prospect, pitching services, or that e-mail will pay a client's invoice. If it's outside the 7-FigurED Sales Process: It's probably not money-generating.

The last item to track, whether or not a task brings you joy, is self-explanatory.

You can do the time study manually with pen and paper or use the spreadsheet I share in the resources for this chapter. Regardless of what way you track, the goal of the time study is to see what you're spending time on. By measuring what is both revenue generating and what brings you joy, you should very quickly be able to see what you could and should be delegating. Any task that is not revenue generating and does not bring you joy can be given to someone else on your team (or added to the job description of who you want to hire).

Let's revisit the two tasks I used earlier:

TIME	TASK	REVENUE GENERATING?	BRINGS YOU JOY?
9:45 A.M.	Answered e-mails	No	No
10:00 A.M.	Wrote a proposal	Yes	Yes

Looking at these tasks through our filters—does it generate revenue, and does it bring you joy?—it's clear that you would want to keep writing proposals but delegate answering e-mails. The clearer you can be in articulating what should be delegated, the better your hiring process will be. In short: Tracking is worth the time and effort.

Your First Hire

Your first hire needs to be for help with operations and admin. Folks love to jump to hire marketing or sales, but in my opinion, that's an ego hire. While it feels nice to grow your social media followers, your business is not going to last if you're late sending invoices and proposals.

Instead, as you approach six figures and beyond in revenue, you need to hire a right hand to help you with the day-to-day running of your business. The first person you hire is going to do a little bit of everything, so you want to hire with that in mind. You want a candidate that has the ability to flex and wear different hats. The person you bring on may be full-time—i.e., an executive assistant (EA)—or you might start with a part-time contractor role, paid hourly—i.e., a virtual assistant (VA). The goal is for this person to take the tasks off your plate that do not generate revenue and/or don't bring you joy. The purpose of having a team is to free you up to work in your Zone of Genius so you can literally do you all day long and generate more revenue and profit as a result.

When you're looking for your right-hand hire, be sure that you hire someone who wants to be a #2. The best executive assistants I have ever had *wanted* to be behind the scenes. A few years ago, when I hosted my annual 7-Figure Educator LIVE event, I wanted to film a reel of my team getting ready. My EA at the time hated the idea. She didn't want to be on camera, like, at all, and only participated because I asked (nicely). My point is that when you hire help—whether it's your first hire or your eighth team member—you want to be clear on that person's role within the organization.

This is one of many reasons why it's crucial to get clear on what you need from the role. That's true in every role you will hire for but can be especially relevant for virtual assistants. Most people don't realize that there are all sorts of specialties within the broader world of VAs. Some are great at automations and overall operations, while others are strictly admin. Others are open to learning and will figure out anything and everything you need. When you understand the responsibilities in advance, you won't hire someone who is not a good fit (like I did the first time around).

Recognize that your first hire is a starting point. Your team will evolve as you grow. In my own business, I started out with a part-time VA to help me with admin tasks and along the way hired VAs with specialties in social media, operations, and events. Today I have a full-time executive assistant and a personal assistant to help me on the daily, because that's the level of support I need to stay in my Zone of Genius and for the rest of my team to stay in theirs so we can collectively execute at our full potential.

VA vs. EA

It's easy to get titles twisted when everyone has their own definition. So here's how I break down the differences between a virtual assistant (VA) and an executive assistant (EA) based on my own experience.

VAs usually work as independent contractors. They take on specific tasks within your business, often tied to their areas of specialty. VAs typically set their own schedules, and because they're contractors, you don't control their time in the same way you would an employee's. That means you may occasionally experience delays, especially since many VAs juggle multiple clients. If your VA lives in a different time zone (especially if they are overseas), you may also need to account for communication lags. The upside is flexibility. VAs tend to be less expensive, and, because they often work hourly, you can scale their hours up or down depending on your business needs.

An EA, on the other hand, is a part-time or full-time employee of your business. While they may complete similar tasks to a VA's, an EA's role goes deeper. They're fully dedicated to your business and can embed themselves in the day-to-day operations as your true right hand. An EA might manage your inbox, gatekeep your calendar, or directly communicate with clients in ways you wouldn't expect a VA to. Because an EA is so intertwined with your operations, you'll need to provide strong onboarding and systems to set them up for success. That's not a drawback—it's simply the level of intentionality required when bringing on someone who will be so deeply connected to how your business runs.

THE HIRING PROCESS

Something I've noticed about the educators I work with: Some of y'all feel hella nervous to hire a VA or help for your team, but you were real chill about hiring a fresh-outta-college teacher to be responsible for 30 kids. Partly that's because of *how* you hire. In schools, we pressure test candidates. We give them sample tasks, we have them student-teach; we review their résumés but value real-life skills more.

We can replicate that same process and set that same bar within our own businesses. As entrepreneurs we can put candidates through the same reps and rigor we did interviewing teachers. In fact, I first learned about this evidence-based approach to hiring, called competency-based hiring, when I was a principal. Unlike traditional recruitment, which tends to value education and experience, competency-based hiring puts the emphasis on what candidates can do in real-world situations.

Within this competency-based framework, a candidate that has the skills but not the specific degree you're looking for would be a better fit than someone who has the degree but not the skills. According to Indeed, employers who use competency-based hiring have improved performance, better retention rates, and experience less bias in hiring practices than those that don't. So, what does competency-based hiring look like in practice? Well, there are five clear steps:

1. Job description
2. Pre-screening
3. First-round interviews
4. Skills test
5. Second-round interviews

STEP 1: JOB DESCRIPTION

To understand who and what you're looking for, you need to first understand what skills and abilities are needed. But before you even get into listing those skills, the job description you create should begin by naming who you are and what you value as a company. This overview gives candidates a glimpse into your culture before they ever meet you, helping them assess whether your business is the kind of place they want to grow with—and whether they might be a fit for your team's rhythm and values. From there, you can move into the role itself. For example, when hiring a virtual assistant, you may want to look for someone who understands the calendar software you use, whether that's iCal, Google Calendar, Acuity, or Calendly. When you write the job description, make sure to articulate the skills, knowledge, and behaviors candidates need in order to be successful in the role.

Ultimately you want the job description to give candidates a big-picture overview of what they'll be doing and what is expected so they can make an informed decision about whether or not to apply. You should include details on when and how the work will be performed (remote or in person), whether you're hiring an employee or a contractor, part-time or full-time, etc. I always include the pay within the job description, because that allows candidates to opt out if you're not aligned on pay. None of that "I didn't learn this job is below my desired pay until the third-round interview" 'ish. (And depending on the size of your business and what state you're in, listing the pay range may be legally required).

When you post the job description online, whether that's on sites like Indeed and LinkedIn, or within groups of your ideal candidates (i.e., VA groups on Facebook), be sure to include a due date for applications so that you know exactly when to move on to the next step.

STEP 2: PRE-SCREENING

After the application due date, the next step is the pre-screening process. This is where you identify three to five nonnegotiables that serve as your baseline evaluation criteria. Think of these as the minimum requirements a candidate must meet in order to be worth your time in an interview. For example, a nonnegotiable might be prior experience working remotely, or proficiency with the specific software your team uses. By setting these standards up front, you ensure that every candidate who makes it to the interview stage already meets the essentials—saving you time, energy, and focus for evaluating the deeper qualities that make someone the right fit.

STEP 3: FIRST-ROUND INTERVIEWS

Next, invite the candidates that make it past your pre-screening process to a 30-minute interview. Ideally you want to meet with six to eight candidates at this stage. (If you have more, you may need to filter down further with another nonnegotiable. If you have fewer, you may want to revisit your nonnegotiables, because you may have been a little too particular.) At this phase, I recommend that you ask three to five core-competency questions.

Think about what the core competencies are for the role that you're hiring for. For example, maybe a core competency for you would be an orientation to customer service. Or perhaps it would be responsiveness or initiative. Whatever those three to five competencies are, I recommend that you draft behavior-style questions to really get to know the candidate's approach or previous experience in those areas. What I mean when I say "behavior-style" is that the answer should tell you how the candidate would behave in a given situation. For example, if you were looking for an orientation to customer service, you could say something like "Tell me about a time you had to work with a difficult client. What was the situation, what did you do or say in response, and what was the outcome?"

Notice that the question forces the candidate to share how they used a particular competency or skill in the past. This is part of why competency-based hiring is so effective. A candidate's past behavior is a better indicator of future behavior than the education and titles on their résumé. The goal at this stage is to end up with two or three candidates that you feel are a good fit to move on to the next step.

STEP 4: SAMPLE TASK OR PROJECT

Once you complete your first-round interviews, it's time to ask the two to three final candidates to complete a sample task or project. What you assign should be something they'll actually do in the role. This is an important step because it gives you insight into each candidate's performance and ability, so be sure to think through what's important. It may be helpful to revisit the nonnegotiables you created for the pre-screening process. Most of the time, the sample task should be relatively simple and take less than an hour to complete. You should also plan to compensate candidates for their time. (I personally offer a flat rate based on how much time I expect the sample task to take.)

For example, a sample task for a customer service agent could be answering an e-mail from a difficult client. For a VA or EA who will manage your calendar, you could present a scenario where they need to cancel all your meetings for a week because you are sick. What you'd be looking for in both cases is how candidates respond to and approach the types of situations and work they'll encounter on your team. When I hired my social media virtual assistant, I gave her a template for one of our recurring social media posts and had her re-create the template. I was looking to see whether she was able to duplicate aspects of our visual branding. I checked over the sample post to see if she used the right font, the right size, the right placement. Before hiring her, I wanted to make sure that she could effectively do a task that frequently comes up within our business.

Most of the time, one to two business days is enough time for candidates to complete the sample task. You want to offer enough time that candidates can do a thorough job while also keeping a sense of urgency in the overall hiring process. When you have the sample tasks back, it's time to move on to the final stage of hiring.

STEP 5: SECOND-ROUND INTERVIEWS

In the second-round interview, you want to review the sample task with your candidates and discuss the specifics of the role you're hiring for, including the technical aspects of the job. This second-round interview should last 45 minutes to an hour and be focused on skill-based questions. For example, when my team was hiring for an operations role, a candidate's résumé listed experience with an automation software we use. Because my team knew that these automations have a tendency to break, we asked the candidate what she would do when one of our automations wasn't working. Specifically, we asked her to walk us through, step-by-step, what she would do in that situation. The point of this question was to understand how she would literally do her job.

Once you go through all five of these steps, you'll have narrowed a whole bunch of applicants down to one, maybe two candidates. At that point, you can make an offer, knowing that you're hiring someone who is likely to be a good fit.

Contractors vs. Employees

While there are important legal and financial differences between hiring someone as an independent contractor or an employee, I want you to plan backward from having a million-dollar business. It's going to be difficult to grow to seven figures and beyond with a team of contractors, because there's not a lot of incentive for independent contractors to be invested in you or your business. Building that way is like operating a school with all substitute teachers. Most educators would never do that, and neither should you as a business owner. Similarly, while W-2 employees can be more expensive than 1099 contractors, you have the benefit of being able to dictate exactly when and how W-2 employees work.

When deciding 1099 versus W-2, a good question to ask yourself is whether the role is permanent or temporary. For example, if you are hiring a VA, is there potential for that person to grow into a full-time role as your executive assistant? Or is the role you are hiring for temporary? What I've found in my own business is that I almost always want to hire a W-2 employee for a role that I know I'll need for the long term, whereas a contractor can be great for a fractional or short-term role.

HOW TO AFFORD YOUR TEAM

When you follow the Profit First methodology (like I suggested way back in Chapter 2), you should always be able to afford to hire what you need. That's because the Profit First methodology helps you save the profit your business makes for future investments, including hiring. That said, if you haven't followed Profit First perfectly or have been under-charging, you may struggle to "afford" hiring help. This is clear feedback that it is time to rerun your numbers and adjust your pricing.

CHAPTER 10 REFLECTION QUESTIONS

1. When you think about your company culture and values, what qualities would your #2 need to embody in order to be a strong extension of you?

2. What three to five nonnegotiables would you set as a baseline for your right-hand hire so you know they can meet your core needs from day one?

3. Looking back at past seasons of overwhelm in your business, what signals would've told you it was time to hire sooner? How can you use those signals moving forward?

4. What fears or hesitations do you have about hiring your right hand, and how can you reframe them into opportunities for strategy, growth, and freedom?

ACTION STEPS

Write at least 3 SOPs:
- Client onboarding
- Client delivery
- Client offboarding

Create an Operations Hub as a library for your SOPs.

Conduct a time study to understand what to delegate.

Hire your right hand by following the five-step hiring process:

1. Write, post, and share a job description

2. Pre-screen candidates

3. Hold first-round interviews

4. Create and assign a sample task or project

5. Host second-round interviews

Then make an offer to the best candidate.

7-FIGURE EDUCATOR RESOURCES

Visit **www.7febook.com/resources** to:

- Review another example of an SOP

- Grab my SOP template

- Watch Episode 55: "Executive Assistants vs. Personal Assistants: How to Build Your Dream Support Team" of the *7-Figure Educator* podcast, where I break down the difference between these two roles and when to hire for each

- Watch Episode 32: "HR for Entrepreneurs: Strategies to Structure a 7-Figure Team with Barbara Mason" of the *7-Figure Educator* podcast, where I sit down with an HR consultant to discuss hiring best practices

Become a Founder

I used to promote an event called Six-Figure Educator Live.

But while I was preparing for the event in 2023, the name just didn't sit right. That's because I realized that achieving six figures in revenue—what I've prepared you to do in this book—is just the basics. That's what is needed for you to take care of yourself, your family, to live a life that's secure.

At the time, I had already expanded past seven figures in revenue. And I had also realized that even a million dollars in revenue didn't allow me to do everything I wanted to do. I couldn't pay my team a living wage *and* benefits *and* be profitable with only a million dollars in revenue.

I needed to reset the goal. So I decided on $10 million instead. (And immediately changed the name of my event to 7-Figure Educator LIVE.) Similarly, when I started writing this book, my goal was to help education consultants like you create a business that generates up to $250,000 annually. But midway through, I realized that I needed to change that goal too.

The same week I finished writing this book, I introduced the 7-FigurED E-Scale Playbook at my 7-Figure Educator LIVE event. This 10-step blueprint shows you how to build, grow, and scale a business. (You can also access my E-Scale course that breaks down the road map for each level in the online resources for this book.) My *ultimate* goal for the educators

I work with isn't $250,000 in revenue. It's not even the million I told y'all we were working toward at the beginning of this book.

It's $5,000,000+.

Now, before you feel bait and switched, let me explain. I realized we educators often have the wrong end goal in mind. That's what I had wrong when I named my live event 6-Figure Educator. I didn't know what I didn't know, but what I realize today is that I had been dreaming small. So I created the 7-FigurED E-Scale to represent the different stages of business, with the end goal of $5,000,000+.

E-SCALE

To understand how I got here, we gotta go back in time. In high school, I played clarinet in the marching band. When we had a concert, all eyes would be on the conductor. Because that's the most important role in any marching band or orchestra, right? The conductor is who sets the pace, who leads the players, who brings it all together in perfect harmony. When I started my career as an educator, my goal was to be the conductor. Maybe that was yours too—we tend to glamorize the role of the school leader within education.

And when I started my business, I brought that mindset with me. I wanted to be the conductor, which in business is the CEO. But when I started stepping into rooms with entrepreneurs who earn seven, eight, nine figures . . . I realized that being a CEO was yet another intermediate step. It was not the end goal. The entrepreneurs earning millions wanted to be someone I didn't even realize existed when I was leading a school, much less when I was playing my clarinet.

Seven-, eight-, and nine-figure entrepreneurs don't want to be the conductor; they want to be the composer—a role that has no equivalent in the world of education. And maybe that's why this goal hasn't occurred to you either.

When a marching band is playing music, the composer has written everything you hear. But the composer doesn't need to be present for the performance, much less the weeks and weeks of practice beforehand. The composer is not in the room where it happens, getting things done. Instead, the composer is somewhere else entirely, because they've done their work already. The composer is a *founder*.

Whether you are pre-revenue or on the cusp of your first seven-figure-revenue year, what you need to know is that you cannot continue growing your business to millions and beyond without adopting a founder's mindset. I would be doing you dirty if I left you thinking that CEO was the end goal, because it doesn't have to be.

Ultimately, this is your business and legacy and wealth that you're building. You get to decide where the goalpost is set. Maybe you want to have a seven-figure business and stop at CEO. You can certainly plan for that. But I don't want you to backward plan from CEO simply because you didn't know founder was available. Because that would be dreaming small.

There is a subtle, but notable, difference between a CEO mindset and a founder mindset. Like an effective principal or superintendent, a CEO prioritizes efficiency. This is where you are focused on driving revenue, creating systems, and developing infrastructure and intellectual property. In many ways, this book has covered the basics of becoming a CEO. When a CEO encounters problems, they work with what they've got.

In contrast, founders are focused on alignment. Their priority is to make sure their business aligns to their vision. If an action or a strategy isn't in alignment with their legacy, it's a no. When a founder encounters a problem, they consider whether it's even worth solving. Founders create resources to solve the issues worth their time. Founders dance with risk and sometimes make big bets to benefit their business based on instinct and self-trust.

Here's a real-life example: One of my mentors has generated more than $100 million over the lifetime of her business. That's nine figures for those who are counting. When I went to an event she was hosting, I could tell she had no idea what the agenda was. I knew because she was asking her team what time lunch was, how long she had to present, details like that. At first, I was like, *How do you not know?* But then I realized she was embodying her role within her company, which was the founder. She wasn't the CEO; she had hired someone else to fill that position. So instead of being involved in the day-to-day, my mentor was the composer. Her job on that day was to pull up and let her team tell her what needed to be done. Because she had already written the score.

Becoming a founder is possible for you too.

This book provides everything you need to build a six-figure education consulting business. In many ways, this is the training ground for you to develop both the vision and the mindset needed to become a founder. Because you can't duplicate what you've never built. You can't lead a team toward clarity you haven't practiced. And you can't grow a business you don't deeply understand.

However, to paraphrase Maya Angelou, when you know better, you can do better. The goal of this book is to give you the knowledge and the tools you need to understand what's ahead. By adopting a founder's mindset from the beginning, you will know what to do next to continue growing and scaling your business—to seven, eight, or nine figures.

And when we become founders, we carve a path wide enough for others to walk too.

Because one founder who looks like us creates room for many more behind us—and if anyone deserves to be a millionaire, it's an educator.

Learn More

At any stage of business, you may need help. Which is why I invite you to continue learning, from me and our community. You can get started for free in our five-day 7-FigurED Business School, or join one of our programs.

If you are generating from $0 to $75,000 annually:

Get LaunchED Consulting Academy will supplement what you learned in this book and help get you consistent four-figure months in your business.

For folks who are generating between $75,000 and $500,000 in annual revenue:

I invite you to check out our Wealthy Black Educator mastermind.

And if your business earned more than $500,000 in revenue last year:

You're eligible for my Lux Mastermind.

Visit our website at **www.7figureeducator.com** to learn more.

Resources

Chapter 1

Ahmed et al., "Why Is There a Higher Rate of Impostor Syndrome Among BIPOC?," Across the Spectrum of Socioeconomics 1, no. 2 (December 2020), https://doi.org/10.5281/zenodo.4310477.

bell hooks, *Sisters of the Yam: Black Women and Self-Recovery*, 2nd ed. (New York: Routledge, 2015).

Chris Wheat, Stacey Chan, and Nicholas Tremper, *Scaling to $1 Million: How Small Businesses Fare by Owner Race and Gender* (New York: JPMorgan Chase Institute, April 2024), https://www.jpmorganchase.com/content/dam/jpmc/jpmorgan-chase-and-co/institute/pdf/1-million-annual-revenues-as-a-small-business-milestone.pdf.

Don Operario and Susan T. Fiske, "Racism Equals Power Plus Prejudice: A Social Psychological Equation for Racial Oppression," in *Confronting Racism: The Problem and the Response*, ed. Jennifer L. Eberhardt and Susan T. Fiske (Thousand Oaks, CA: Sage, 1998), 33–53.

Clance, Pauline R., and Suzanne A. Imes, "The Imposter Phenomenon in High Achieving Women: Dynamics and Therapeutic Intervention," *Psychotherapy: Theory, Research & Practice* 15, no. 3 (1978): 241–247.

Guante, "How to Explain White Supremacy to a White Supremacist," Guante, March 17, 2016 (new version of video February 12, 2017), https://guante.info/2016/03/17/how-to-explain-white-supremacy-to-a-white-supremacist-new-video/.

Melissa Houston, "The Wealth Gap: Why We Need More Women Making Millions," *Forbes*, March 8, 2025, https://

www.forbes.com/sites/melissahouston/2025/03/08/
the-wealth-gap-why-we-need-more-women-making-millions/.

Chapter 2

"401(k) Retirement Savings Calculator," Bankrate, accessed September 29,
2025, https://www.bankrate.com/retirement/401-k-calculator/.

Andre M. Perry, Manann Donoghoe, and Hannah Stephens, "Closing the
Black Employer Gap: Insights from the Latest Data on Black-Owned
Businesses," Brookings Institution, February 15, 2024, https://www
.brookings.edu/articles/closing-the-black-employer-gap-insights-from
-the-latest-data-on-black-owned-businesses/.

Charisse Jones, "For Faces Behind Aunt Jemima, Uncle Ben's and Cream
of Wheat, Life Transcended Stereotype," *USA Today*, updated July
12, 2020, https://www.usatoday.com/story/money/2020/07/10/real
-people-behind-aunt-jemima-uncle-ben-cream-of-wheat/3285054001/.

Clay Risen, "Wally Amos, Enterprising Creator of Famous Amos Cookies,
Dies at 88," *New York Times*, updated August 17, 2024, https://www
.nytimes.com/2024/08/14/business/wally-amos-dead.html.

"Cost of Living Index by State 2025," World Population Review,
accessed September 29, 2025, https://worldpopulationreview.com/
state-rankings/cost-of-living-index-by-state.

Crystal L. Hoyt, "Inspirational or Self-Deflating: The Role of Self-
Efficacy in Elite Role Model Effectiveness," *Social Psychological
and Personality Science* 4, no. 3 (May 15, 2013): 290–98, https://doi
.org/10.1177/1948550612455066.

Katie Hawkinson, "Wally Amos, Pioneering Creator of Iconic Cookie Brand
Famous Amos, Dies Aged 88," *Independent*, August 14, 2024, https://
www.independent.co.uk/news/world/americas/wally-amos-dead
-famous-amos-cookies-b2596512.html.

Opher Ganel, "What's the Difference: Self-Employed vs. Employee?,"
Wealthtender, accessed September 29, 2025, https://wealthtender
.com/insights/employee-vs-self-employed/.

Robert T. Kiyosaki, *Rich Dad's Cashflow Quadrant: Guide to Financial Freedom*
(New York: Plata Publishing, 2011).

Rüdiger J. Seitz and Raymond F. Paloutzian, "Beliefs Made It into Science, Believe It or Not," *Function* 4, no. 6 (September 2023): zqad049, https://doi.org/10.1093/function/zqad049.

"Salary & Benefits," NYC Public Schools, accessed September 29, 2025, https://teachnyc.net/your-career/salary-and-benefits.

"S&P 500 (^GSPC) Historical Data," Yahoo Finance, accessed September 29, 2025, https://finance.yahoo.com/quote/%5EGSPC/history/.

"SEP Contribution Limits (Including Grandfathered SARSEPs)," Internal Revenue Service, accessed September 29, 2025, https://www.irs.gov/retirement-plans/plan-participant-employee/sep-contribution-limits-including-grandfathered-sarseps.

"Starting Teacher Pay: Starting Teacher Salaries," National Education Association, accessed September 29, 2025, https://www.nea.org/resource-library/educator-pay-and-student-spending-how-does-your-state-rank/starting-teacher.

Toni Morrison, commencement address, Sarah Lawrence College, Bronxville, NY, May 28, 1988.

"Trademark, Patent, or Copyright," U.S. Patent and Trademark Office, accessed September 29, 2025, https://www.uspto.gov/trademarks/basics/trademark-patent-copyright.

Chapter 3

"Amazon Startup Story," Fundable, accessed September 29, 2025, https://www.fundable.com/learn/startup-stories/amazon.

Clay Risen, "Gloria Richardson, Uncompromising Civil Rights Advocate, Dies at 99," *New York Times*, July 18, 2021, https://www.nytimes.com/2021/07/18/us/gloria-richardson-dead.html.

Dwayne Spradlin, "The Power of Defining the Problem," *Harvard Business Review*, September 25, 2012, https://hbr.org/2012/09/the-power-of-defining-the-prob.

Food Allergy Facts and Statistics for the U.S. (Food Allergy Research and Education, April 2024), https://www.foodallergy.org/sites/default/files/2024-07/FARE%20Food%20Allergy%20Facts%20and%20Statistics_April2024.pdf.

Gay Hendricks, *The Big Leap: Conquer Your Hidden Fear and Take Life to the Next Level* (New York: HarperCollins, 2009).

Geri Stengel, "Black Korean Female Founder Overcomes VC Bias to Disrupt CPG Industry," updated November 20, 2023, *Forbes*, https://www .forbes.com/sites/geristengel/2023/11/15/black-korean-female -founder-overcomes-vc-bias-to-disrupt-cpg-industry/.

"Not 'Just' a Teacher," Research for Better Teaching, accessed September 29, 2025, https://www.rbteach.com/resources/blog/library/55.

Chapter 4

"Bloom's Taxonomy," Stearns Center for Teaching and Learning, George Mason University, accessed September 29, 2025, https://stearnscenter .gmu.edu/knowledge-center/course-and-curriculum-redesign/ blooms-taxonomy/.

Clay Risen, "Jack Daniel's Embraces a Hidden Ingredient: Help From a Slave," *New York Times*, June 25, 2016, https://www.nytimes .com/2016/06/26/dining/jack-daniels-whiskey-nearis-green-slave .html.

Fred Minnick, "Jack Daniel's Named Most Valuable Spirits Brand in World," November 7, 2022, https://www.fredminnick.com/2022/11/07/ jack-daniels-named-most-valuable-spirits-brand-in-world/.

"How Uncle Nearest Founder Fawn Weaver Built a Billion-Dollar Whiskey Business," *Forbes*, YouTube video, 15:14, May 28, 2024, https://www .youtube.com/watch?v=XtH9o_UxqEc.

Phoenix Scholar Magazine 1, no. 3 (Summer 2018), University of Phoenix, accessed September 29, 2025, https://www.phoenix.edu/research/ publications/phoenix-scholar/vol-1-issue-3.html.

Richard Pérez-Peña, "John G. Sperling, For-Profit College Pioneer, Dies at 93," *New York Times*, August 25, 2014, https://www.nytimes .com/2014/08/26/us/john-g-sperling-for-profit-college-pioneer -dies-at-93.html.

"Teacher Evaluation: A Metric for Performance," SlideServe, accessed September 29, 2025, https://www.slideserve.com/erma/ teacher-evaluation-a-metric-for-performance.

Chapter 5

Aimee L. Dennis, "Impact of Response to Intervention on Achievement" (EdD diss., University of Texas at Tyler, 2023), https://scholarworks .uttyler.edu/cgi/viewcontent.cgi?params=/context/education_grad/ article/1006/&path_info=Impact_of_Response_to_Intervention_on Achievement.pdf.

Chapter 6

Anna Rostomyan, "The Value of Active Listening as a Component of EQ," *Psychology Today*, updated November 5, 2024, https://www .psychologytoday.com/us/blog/emotions-in-our-lives/202411/ the-value-of-active-listening-as-a-component-of-eq.

Devon Nir, "Are Racially Isolated Black Teachers More Likely to Leave Their Jobs?," Thomas B. Fordham Institute, August 29, 2024, https://fordhaminstitute.org/national/commentary/ are-racially-isolated-black-teachers-more-likely-leave-their-jobs.

"Michael Jordan Didn't Make Varsity—At First," *Newsweek* Special Edition, updated April 24, 2016, https://www.newsweek.com/ missing-cut-382954.

Shane Safir, *The Listening Leader: Creating the Conditions for Equitable School Transformation* (San Francisco: Jossey-Bass, 2017).

Shane Safir, "Learning to Listen," ASCD, May 1, 2017, https://www.ascd .org/el/articles/learning-to-listen.

Tema Okun, "White Supremacy Culture Characteristics," accessed September 29, 2025, https://www.whitesupremacyculture.info/ characteristics.html.

Chapter 7

"ConvertKit," Sacra.com, accessed September 29, 2025, https://sacra.com/c/ convertkit/.

Matt Stevens, "How Much Does It Cost to See Beyoncé? It Depends," *New York Times*, May 15, 2025, https://www.nytimes.com/2025/05/15/arts/music/beyonce-cowboy-carter-tour-ticket-prices.html.

Nathan Barry, "The Ladders of Wealth Creation: A Step-by-Step Roadmap to Building Wealth," December 3, 2019, https://nathanbarry.com/wealth-creation/.

"Value-Based Pricing," Wall Street Prep, updated July 17, 2024, https://www.wallstreetprep.com/knowledge/value-based-pricing/.

Chapter 8

"Why Our Attention Spans Are Shrinking, with Gloria Mark, PhD," February 8, 2023, in *Speaking of Psychology*, podcast, produced by the American Psychological Association, https://www.apa.org/news/podcasts/speaking-of-psychology/attention-spans.

Chapter 9

Eric Belcher and Leo Feler, "Research: What Explains the 'Vibecession'?," *Harvard Business Review*, January 30, 2025, https://hbr.org/2025/01/research-what-explains-the-vibecession.

Holz et al., "Eliminating Customer Experience Pain Points in Complex Customer Journeys Through Smart Service Solutions," *Psychology and Marketing* 41, no. 3 (March 2024): 592–609, https://doi.org/10.1002/mar.21938.

Jim Collins, "The Flywheel Effect," JimCollins.com, accessed September 29, 2025, https://www.jimcollins.com/concepts/the-flywheel.html.

"Launch of Savage X Fenty—Lingerie by Rihanna," Shorty Awards, accessed September 29, 2025, https://shortyawards.com/11th/launch-of-savage-x-fenty-lingerie-by-rihanna.

"Our Values, Activism, and Mission," Ben & Jerry's, accessed September 29, 2025, https://www.benjerry.com/values.

RAIN Group, "How Many Touchpoints Does It Take to Make a Sale?," *RAIN Group Sales Blog*, accessed December 13, 2025. https://www.rainsalestraining.com/blog/how-many-touchpoints-does-it-take-to-make-a-sale.

Ryan Pendell, "Customer Brand Preference and Decisions: Gallup's 70/30 Principle," Gallup, updated September 30, 2022, https://www.gallup.com/workplace/398954/customer-brand-preference-decisions-gallup-principle.aspx.

"The Subconscious Mind of the Consumer (and How to Reach It)," Harvard Business School, January 13, 2003, https://www.library.hbs.edu/working-knowledge/the-subconscious-mind-of-the-consumer-and-how-to-reach-it.

Vinnie Wong, "Social Media Demographics 2025," *Piktochart*, updated June 24, 2025, https://piktochart.com/blog/social-media-demographics-2025/; Mahnoor Sheikh, "Social Media Demographics to Inform Your 2025 Strategy," Sprout Social, accessed July 8, 2025, https://sproutsocial.com/insights/new-social-media-demographics/.

Chapter 10

Andre M. Perry, Manann Donoghoe, and Hannah Stephens, "Closing the Black Employer Gap: Insights from the Latest Data on Black-Owned Businesses," Brookings Institution, February 15, 2024, https://www.brookings.edu/articles/closing-the-black-employer-gap-insights-from-the-latest-data-on-black-owned-businesses/.

Angela Petulla, "2024 Small Business Revenue Statistics," AltLINE, updated April 9, 2025, https://altline.sobanco.com/small-business-revenue-statistics/.

Oprah, "The Powerful Lesson Maya Angelou Taught Oprah," October 19, 2011, clip from *Oprah's Lifeclass*, https://www.oprah.com/oprahs-lifeclass/the-powerful-lesson-maya-angelou-taught-oprah-video.

Robert McAllister, "Black-Owned Businesses in the U.S. See Significant Growth but Still Face Disparities," NCHStats, February 14, 2025, https://nchstats.com/black-owned-businesses-in-us/.

Simon Bedard, "Key Person Risk: What Is It Costing Your Business?," *Forbes*, January 10, 2024, https://www.forbes.com/councils/forbesbusinesscouncil/2024/01/10/key-person-risk-what-is-it-costing-your-business/.

"What Is Competency-Based Recruitment?," Indeed, updated December 4, 2025, https://www.indeed.com/hire/c/info/competency-based-recruitment.

Index

A

B

C

G

H

K

L

M

N

O

P

Q

R

S

Y

Z

Acknowledgments

*"For I know the plans I have for you," declares
the Lord, "plans to prosper you and not to harm
you, plans to give you hope and a future."*

— JEREMIAH 29:11

This scripture is tattooed on my foot, not as an aesthetic choice, but as a covenant. A reminder that even when I cannot see the full picture, the plan is already complete. This book is another living, breathing affirmation of that truth.

The idea for this book came to me in 2019, not as a clear vision, but as a knowing. I didn't know what the book would be about. I didn't know the title. I didn't know the publisher. But I knew, with certainty, that a book was coming and that preparation was required. So I did what I've always done when faith and discipline meet: I prepared before clarity arrived.

During my second year in my doctoral program, I created an independent study and made my final assignment a book proposal. At the time, it felt audacious and premature. But looking back, it was obedience. That independent study became a sacred rehearsal. I interviewed authors. I interviewed editors. I studied the craft, the business, and the responsibility of authorship. I planted seeds years before I would see fruit. God knew what was coming long before I did, and this book is proof that when you move in alignment, timing reveals itself.

To Meghan Stevenson, my editorial collaborator and book fairy godmother . . . thank you for walking this road with me hand in hand. From the earliest stages of the proposal to the final words on these pages, your steady presence mattered more than you know. Thank you for the warm headshakes, the thoughtful questions, the patience with my many e-mails and text messages, and the care you brought to every single step of this journey. You helped bring the heart of this work to life.

To my agents at Folio Literary Management, Steve Troha and Eloise Davenport, thank you for championing this book from the very first read. Thank you for seeing the vision clearly, for believing in the message, and for advocating with excellence and integrity. Every author deserves representation that believes as deeply as they do, and I do not take that gift lightly.

To Hay House, thank you for taking a bet on a book that boldly declares educators should be millionaires. Thank you for honoring a message that disrupts outdated narratives and expands what is possible for those who have long been underpaid, undervalued, and underestimated. To my editors, Melody Guy and Allison Adler, thank you for your guidance, discernment, and partnership throughout this process. Your stewardship of this work helped ensure it reached the world with clarity, care, and conviction.

To Skye High Interactive, the designers who gave me the cover of my dreams. Thank you for making the impossible possible. You somehow managed to make me fall in love with an apple by wrapping it in money, and that still makes me smile. More than design, you captured metaphor, movement, and meaning in a single visual. That is no small feat.

To Amy Porterfield, thank you for your wisdom, generosity, and steady guidance throughout this book journey. Thank you for creating the space where I could say out loud something that once scared me: I want to be a *New York Times* bestseller. I was able to say it because I saw it through you. Your belief helped strengthen my own, and that matters.

To Luvvie Ajayi Jones and the Bestselling Book Mastermind team, thank you for everything you poured into me. Your transparency illuminated the path of traditional publishing and reminded me that excellence and integrity can coexist at the highest levels. Your investment changed how I moved through this process.

To my business mentors, Lamar and Ronnie Tyler, thank you for your mentorship, your wisdom, and your unwavering support. You've helped shape not just how I build businesses, but how I think about legacy, leadership, and scale.

To Olympic Renaissance High School, Reid Park Academy, Ranson IB Middle School, and the Project LIFT community, thank you for shaping the educator and leader I am today. Every hallway, classroom, student, and colleague contributed to the foundation that made this book possible. I carry those experiences with me in every room I enter.

To the 7-Figure Educator team, thank you for being ten toes down in bringing our mission to life. Your commitment, excellence, and belief ensure that every educator we serve can see their next level reflected back to them through the experiences we deliver. This book is an extension of the work we do together every day.

To the 7-Figure Educator community, thank you for trusting us as your partner in growth. To every client who has attended a webinar, joined a Business School, enrolled in a program, or shown up at an event . . . THANK YOU. To the OGs who've been rocking with me since Six-Figure Educator

2022, I see you. I don't take your trust for granted, and we are not done yet ;-).

To my family and friends, thank you for your unconditional love, patience, and grace. Thank you for understanding delayed replies, long seasons of focus, and moments of absence. Your support held me up more than you know.

And last but not least, I want to thank me.

I want to thank me for believing in me, especially in the seasons when the vision was bigger than the evidence. I want to thank myself for the sacrifices, the long nights, the early mornings, and the quiet discipline that no one clapped for. I want to thank myself for being intentional about joy, about creating moments of rest, laughter, and life in the middle of building because sustainability is not accidental. It's a choice.

I want to thank me for doing the hard mindset work. For looking fear square in the face and not letting it drive my car. Acknowledging it, but putting it firmly in the backseat. I want to thank me for making decisions that stretched me, decisions that required courage over comfort, alignment over approval. This journey has reminded me that mindset is not a destination, it's a daily practice. And so I thank me for consistently choosing to do the work, again and again, even when it was uncomfortable.

I didn't just write this book, I became the woman who could.

About the Author

Dr. Erica Jordan-Thomas is CEO and Founder of EJT Education Group, a business development company on a mission to shift the power dynamics in education and disrupt the racial wealth gap by providing high-performing Black educators with the tools to grow a seven-figure education consulting business. She holds a bachelor of arts degree from The Ohio State University, a master's degree in instructional leadership from Relay Graduate School of Education, and a doctorate in education leadership from Harvard Graduate School of Education.

HAY HOUSE TITLES OF RELATED INTEREST

WHAT DO YOU NEED?:
How Women of Color Can Take Ownership of
Their Careers to Accelerate Their Path to Success
by Lauren Wesley Wilson

THINK LIKE A BOSS:
Stop Playing Small and Start Thinking Big
by Maggie Colette

TWO WEEKS NOTICE:
Find the Courage to Quit Your Job,
Make More Money, Work Where You Want,
and Change the World
by Amy Porterfield

BUILDING YOUR MONEY MACHINE:
How to Get Your Money to Work Harder
for You Than You Did for It!
by Mel H. Abraham

All of the above are available at your local bookstore,
or may be ordered by visiting:

Hay House USA: www.hayhouse.com*
Hay House Australia: www.hayhouse.com.au
Hay House UK: www.hayhouse.co.uk
Hay House India: www.hayhouse.co.in

We hope you enjoyed this Hay House book. If you'd like to receive our online catalog featuring additional information on Hay House books and products, or if you'd like to find out more about the Hay Foundation, please contact:

Hay House LLC, P.O. Box 5100, Carlsbad, CA 92018-5100
(760) 431-7695 or (800) 654-5126
www.hayhouse.com® • www.hayfoundation.org

———

Published in Australia by:
Hay House Australia Publishing Pty Ltd
18/36 Ralph St., Alexandria NSW 2015
Phone: +61 (02) 9669 4299
www.hayhouse.com.au

Published in the United Kingdom by:
Hay House UK Ltd
1st Floor, Crawford Corner,
91–93 Baker Street, London W1U 6QQ
Phone: +44 (0)20 3927 7290
www.hayhouse.co.uk

Published in India by:
Hay House Publishers (India) Pvt Ltd
Muskaan Complex, Plot No. 3,
B-2, Vasant Kunj, New Delhi 110 070
Phone: +91 11 41761620
www.hayhouse.co.in

———

Let Your Soul Grow

Experience life-changing transformation—one video
at a time—with guidance from the world's leading experts.

www.healyourlifeplus.com